MY BROTHER'S KEEPER

Written by

JONATHAN ARRINGTON

FREE?, July 2024

Copyright by Jonathan Arrington

For any inquires contact

scripts.jonathanarrington@gmail.com

or

freefilmworks@gmail.com

ISBN: 979-8-9907679-0-4
ISBN: 979-8-9907679-1-1

To my Mother

For loving me even when loving herself seemed
impossible.

To my Sister

For being my number one supporter and protecting me
through the years.

And to my Uncle

Whose presence is felt each and everyday, may you
rest in peace

I hope these words ignite your journey to recovery,
Lord knows it has ignited mine.

First, over BLACK we hear...

Two voices. Young, vulnerable, and passionate.

>   BOY (O.S.)
>   Michelle?

>   MICHELLE
>   Yes?

>   BOY
>   If you loved me today, and the day before,
>   will you love me tomorrow?

>   MICHELLE
>   Of course, for eternity and everyday after.

The boy laughs.

>   MICHELLE
>   What?

>   JUNIOR
>   You sound like a punk.

>   MICHELLE
>   You know what.

They laugh again, horse playing in the darkness,
both voices although different share one common
emotion, love. Their laughter fades.

Then...

>   FADE IN:

EXT. SAVANNAH ST. WASHINGTON, D.C. - DAY

A bright and clear, Savannah St. day. The heatwaves
have begun to rise from the asphalt.

An airplane roars above. Apartments are lined up on
the right side of the street along with cars of all
makes and models on their respective sides. Across
the street from the apartments are the woods and a
newly built playground.

The street extends far beyond what the eye can see;
it is or at least appears to be infinite.

A figure is seen in the distance walking towards us.
In due time, our clear image of Savannah St. is
tarnished by...

... a zombie

Or perhaps a man, his tall frame hidden under the
deep hutch in his back. He is round in shape,
disgruntled, oblivious to the world around him. He
is dressed in an old military jacket (it is
authentic; think Desert Storm era) it is tight on
him as he has outgrown it with time.

A brown paper bag with a beer inside occupies one
hand, a rusted silver hook has replaced his opposite
hand. He staggers slowly down the street talking to
himself in two distinct voices.

                    VET
            (Think Drill Sergeant/ Commanding
            Officer)
        What makes the grass grow? What makes it
        grow Private, come on tell me what makes
        the grass grow?

He switches voices.

                    VET
        BLOOD SERGEANT!

He switches back.

                    VET
          I CAN'T HEAR YOU!!

He switches again.

                    VET
          I said Blood Sergeant.

He takes a long drink from his beer, as if it is the
last drop of water in his canteen.

He switches to a voice we haven't heard, not of a
soldier but as something far more complex, a human.

                    VET
          Blood makes the grass grow. But we in the
          desert, grass don't grow in the desert, we
          got the blood, blood over here, blood over
          there, we all bleeding sarge, the grass
          just ain't growin, when the grass gon come
          sarge? Where it at?

He chuckles to himself but this chuckle becomes a
full-on hyena like cackle. We HEAR the laughter of
some kids off screen intensifying as it gets closer
to us.

A group of kids (adolescents, ranging from 10 to 13
years of age) run past the drunken VET. One of the
kids accidentally knocks the beer out of his hands.

The contents from the can spill onto the concrete.
The VET looks at his can spilling as if it is one of
his fallen comrades.

He staggers over to the can getting on his hands and
knees. Crawling over to the beer lowering his face
to the point where he is now slurping the beer up
from the concrete. The laughter continues in the
distance.

CUT TO:

EXT. SAVANNAH ST. - BACKSIDE OF APARTMENT- DAY

The backside of the apartment complex is more of a
wide open space with trees, grass, and a few parked
cars.

All of the kids are running together down the
street. They begin to scatter, deviating from the
street and running in different directions.

We focus on one of the kids, MICHELLE (13 years old,
black) hauling ass down a sidewalk that leads to the
backside of the complex.

MICHELLE makes her way down the path and takes cover
behind a tree. She is trying to regain her breath.
She peeks around the tree to see if the coast is
clear. It is.

She abandons her cover, tip toeing to another tree.
Her head is on a constant swivel, never looking in
any one direction for too long. She gets to the
other tree and looks out again to see where people
are.

Suddenly...

A boy (around the same age as Michelle) drops out of
the tree with a belt in hand. MICHELLE turns but it
is too late, the boy has already swung his belt,
hitting MICHELLE on the leg.

                    BOY 1
          Aye y'all Michelle's it.

All of the kids come out from their creative and
obscure hiding places and are now forming a circle
around the two.

                    MICHELLE
          Why you hit me so hard?

                    BOY 1
          Man up.

                    MICHELLE
          Keep that same energy. I'm about to beat
          you like a slave.

                    BOY 1
          You the slave.

                    MICHELLE
          I'm nobody's slave, your mamas a slave.

                    BOY 1
          Don't talk about my mama.

                    MICHELLE
          Just give me the damn belt.

The boy hands her the belt and MICHELLE snatches it
out of his hands.

The kids circle around MICHELLE moving methodically
around her. She closes her eyes and begins to
count...

                    MICHELLE
          10,9,8...

The game has been initiated. The kids fan out. When
she gets to ONE, she opens her eyes and spots the
boy that had hit her. She runs behind him and is
constantly getting closer. He tries to evade her by
making sharp turns and cuts, but MICHELLE is just
too fast.

She catches him and starts wailing on him, giving
him a barrage of hits along his back and legs. He
screams and curls up in the fetal position while the
other kids circle around and laugh.

                    MICHELLE
               (Dropping the belt on him)
          You're it.

                                        CUT TO:

EXT. SAVANNAH ST. - DAY - MOMENTS LATER

MICHELLE is sitting on a median rail alongside her
best friend, RANAE, and other kids from the
neighborhood. All of them eating ice sticks or
drinking Caprisuns. They are looking at the cars
driving by.

                    BOY 1
          Ouuu look at that one!

                    BOY 2
          That's mine right there.

                    BOY 1
          You don't even know what type of car that
          is.

                    BOY 2
          I'm gonna find out and when I do I'm going
          to get it.

Another car drives past.

                    BOY 2
          Never mind I want that one.

                    BOY 1
          You already picked yours.

                    RANAE

Well y'all can stop arguing now cause it's
mine, and when I make it big, I'm buying it
for my mama.

                    BOY 1
She just gonna trade it for drugs anyway.

The kids start laughing.

                    GIRL 1
That's wild as shit.

                    MICHELLE
 Why would you say that?

                    RANAE
I don't know why you keep talking to me,
ugly ass boy.

                    BOY 1
I ain't ugly, you ugly. Looking like your
dad and shit.

                    RANAE
You don't even know what your daddy look
like.

The kids laugh again. This time MICHELLE reaches out
her hand, giving RANAE a high five.

Police sirens sound off in the background and kids
begin to take notice as it comes closer.

                    MICHELLE
OH SHIT LOOK!

A tinted out BLACK IMPALA zooms past with several
police cars chasing fast behind it. They cheer it
on.

                    BOY 1
Go nigga go!!

A boy throws a rock in the direction of the cop
cars.

                    RANAE
          Oh shit he got out the car.

                    BOY 2
          What he stop for?

GUNSHOTS ring out in the distance, a shootout has
ensued. The kids fan out.

A CLOSE UP on the rail reveals a hole created by a
stray bullet. Through the hole we see the kids
running away, upright and laughing, completely
oblivious to how close they were to death.

EXT. SAVANNAH ST. PLAYGROUND - DAY - CONTINUOUS

We track through different groups of kids. One group
has all of their shoes in the middle, reciting the
"bubble gum, bubble gum in a dish" rhyme, to
determine who is going to be it.

A group of boys have began an intense game of
contact football.

RANAE is seen on a swing kissing a boy on the lips.
We track to MICHELLE who is sitting next to a boy
who is trying to kiss her.

                    MICHELLE
          Back up.

                    BOY 1
          I thought you were my girl, aint that what
          girls supposed to do.

                    MICHELLE
          Well not this one.

The boy sucks his teeth.

                    BOY 1
              (Under his breath)
     I knew I should've just talked to Sarah.

                    MICHELLE
     What? Yeah, that's what I thought.

We leave them and move to the neighboring slide
where a group of kids have surrounded a boy who is
at the top of the slide.

All of their eyes are glued on this boy's face, he's
animated and excited to tell this story.

                    BOY 1
     So we sitting there and next thing you know
     eight police cars come ballin down the
     street, I ain't never seen no shit like
     that. They had swat team and everything.

                    BOY 2
     DAMNNN they had the SWAT TEAM!!

                    GIRL 1
     How you just gonna lie like that?

                    BOY 3
     Please let the man finish his story god
     damn.

                    BOY 1
     Thank you! There was eight cars and two big
     swat trucks. The cars go by and we all
     cheering and next thing you know the dude
     that was gettin chased hop out the car with
     the AR and just started spraying shit.

                    BOY 2
     How you know it was an AR?

                    BOY 1
     Cause I heard it.

                    BOY 3
          Did it sound like this?

He imitates the sounds of an AR, with his mouth.

                    BOY 3
          Or was it like. BOW. BOW. BOW . BOW?

                    BOY 1
          I don't know the first one.

                    BOY 3
          What you mean you don't know? Wasn't you
          there?

                    GIRL 1
          He was prolly the first one gone with his
          scared ass.

The kids all laugh.

                    BOY 1
          Fuck y'all I know what I heard.

                                        CUT TO:

EXT. SAVANNAH ST. - CONTINUOUS

A woman walking down the sidewalk. We don't see her
face, just the quickness of her walk. She gets to
the edge of the sidewalk and walks onto the street,
in the distance we see the children. We RACK FOCUS
back and forth between the woman's leg and the
children in the distance.

                    WOMAN
          MICHELLE!!!

All the kids turn around to look at her, except
MICHELLE. The woman screams her name again. All the
kids now saying it in unison:

"oouuuuuuuuuuu"

                    MICHELLE
          What?

                    WOMAN
          GIRL DON'T WHAT ME! Come on its time to
          eat.

                    MICHELLE
          Please ma five more minutes.

                    RUTH
          DON'T MAKE ME REPEAT MYSELF, AND GO GET
          YOUR BROTHER.

EXT. SAVANNAH ST. PLAYGROUND - CONTINUOUS

                    BOY 1
          Man, yo mamma sound scary as hell.

                    MICHELLE
          Extra for no reason.

                    RANAE
          You better go, before she keep you in the
          house all summer.

                    MICHELLE
          I'll see y'all later.

MICHELLE gives RANAE a hug and walks off.

                    BOY 1
          Where my hug at?

MICHELLE flicks him off holding up her middle finger
while the kids laugh.

EXT. SAVANNAH ST. WOODS - CONTINUOUS

A boy (12) small in stature, walking away from us, big stick in hand swiping through the tall grass, he wanders through this terrain with familiarity. His t-shirt, stained with a combination of blood and dirt.

The grass around him starts to rustle, he looks in the direction of the noise.

A stray cat comes out of the grass, eyeing the boy. They both look at each other. He takes a step towards the cat but it begins backing up. He stops and reaches in his pocket, he pulls out a crushed up granola bar, and places it down for the cat.

The cat walks towards him, eating the granola bar, JUNIOR stoops to the cat's level giving him more food, and petting him. A smile creeps on his face, two outcasts enjoying each other, no longer alone.

In the distance....

                    MICHELLE (O.S.)
          JUNIOR! JUNIOR!

He looks in her direction. His smile disappears into a blank emotionless gaze. This moment is now a memory.

                    MICHELLE
          Let's go dinner about to be ready.

JUNIOR starts walking towards her. The cat follows.

                    MICHELLE
          What happened to your face?

JUNIOR doesn't respond, he just keeps walking.

                    MICHELLE

                    I asked you a question and get this cat out
                    of here. I told you to stop feeding these
                    cats.

She shoos the cat away and it scurries off.

                         MICHELLE
                    I'm going to ask you this one more time,
                    what happened to your face?

JUNIOR does not respond as they continue walking
towards their house.

INT. THE FAMILY HOUSE- KITCHEN - EVENING

MICHELLE and JUNIOR are standing in front of their
mother RUTH (mid 40s), she towers over both of them,
their gazes fixed to the ground.

The mothers tone overpowers the boiling oil in the
kitchen.

                         RUTH
                      (Stern)
                    Now I'm not going to ask you again, who did
                    this to you?

JUNIOR is quiet, still focused on his spot on the
ground.

She takes a couple steps towards him, grabbing his
face, slowly pulling it up towards her revealing...

...the scars on JUNIOR'S face. His eyes slightly
tearing up. He snatches his head away.

                         RUTH
                    Did you fight back?

JUNIOR remains quiet, his gaze falls back to his
feet, staring at the floor, his answer revealed
through the silence.

                    RUTH
               (Disappointed/Stern)
          We'll deal with this when your dad gets
          home.

JUNIOR leaves the room and MICHELLE tries to follow
him.

                    RUTH
          Michelle.

She stops and turns back around, her mother gestures
to her to have a seat at the table. She sits, her
mother takes a couple steps toward her.

                    RUTH
          And where were you?

                    MICHELLE
          I was with Ranae.

                    RUTH
          So you was playing while your brother was
          getting his ass whooped.

                    MICHELLE
          I aint his bodyguard.

                    RUTH
          Don't get smart with me.

MICHELLE sits back in her chair. Her mother bends,
meeting her eye to eye.

                    RUTH

The next time someone is fighting your
brother and I find out that you didn't do
anything then I'm gonna beat you my damn
self. From now on wherever he goes you go
and if something happens then you better
use those fists, pick up a rock, anything
and beat the hell out of anyone who messes
with your brother. Y'all ain't babies
anymore. If something happens to me or your
father the only thing you will have in this
world is your brother.

MICHELLE continues looking down.

                    RUTH
Do you hear me talking to you?

                    MICHELLE
Yes m'am.

                    RUTH
Go wash up. Your father should be here
soon.

MICHELLE walks away towards the bathroom.

INT. BATHROOM - EVENING

JUNIOR is lightly tapping rubbing alcohol on his
wounds it burns, the sting making him wince.

MICHELLE walks in and grabs her wash cloth, they
both stand in the mirror.

                    MICHELLE
When are you gonna be a man?

A beat of contemplation, MICHELLE is looking JUNIOR
in his eyes, he tries to ignore her, he's heard this
before.

                    MICHELLE
          I'm tired of mom getting on me about
          protecting you. Stop acting like you're
          weak.

                    JUNIOR
          I'm not weak.

                    MICHELLE
          Your face says otherwise. If you're scared
          just say that.

JUNIOR slams the washcloth down and storms out of
the bathroom.

INT. THE FAMILY HOUSE- KITCHEN - DAY

Their mother prepares the table for dinner. She
places the chicken, collards and cornbread on the
table. She mixes together some fruit-punch Kool-Aid
which she puts on the table as well.

Finally she sits on the other end of the dinner
table and waits.

Keys begin to JINGLE, the door opens.

Two men walk in, they are talking, we do not see
their faces but hear their boots thumping against
the hardwood floor.

                    EARL
          I ain't gonna keep listening to that man. I
          showed up did the work and he talkin bout I
          can't get my money.

                    HAY
          Don't worry about that Earl.

                    EARL SR.

I ain't worried. I got some land down the
country.

                    HAY
What you gonna do with land?

Both men are now in the kitchen. EARL (mid 40s) the
father of MICHELLE and JUNIOR. He is a built man of
average height. His hands know nothing but work, his
mind focused only on the moment in time he is
occupying.

He walks past his wife and straight to the fridge
where he pulls out a can of Budweiser. HAY sits at
an open seat at the table.

                    HAY
How you doing Ruth?

                    RUTH
I'm good Hay, how about you?

                    HAY
Same ole; same ole.

                    EARL
             (To Hay)
You want a beer?

                    HAY
You already know.

He tosses a beer over to Hay who opens the beer
almost instantly. Earl takes his seat at the head of
the table.

                    EARL
Ima grow tobacco.

                    HAY
You ont know nothing about no damn tobacco.
What you know about tobacco?

                    EARL
          Henry got big land down there he know what
          he doing. Makin good money too.

                    HAY
          Your brother Henry?

                    EARL
          Yeah that's what I said. He got sum land
          waitin for me.... Baby tell'm bout the land
          down the country

                    RUTH
          I know y'all better wash yall hands at
          least. I know that much.

Earl and Hay look at each other and laugh.

                    RUTH
          You ain't give me a kiss, a hug or nothing
          and you going on talking about some land.

                    EARL
          You see how she do me.

He gets up and walks over to her, bends down and
kisses her on the cheek, then on the lips. He stops
and goes to wash his hand.

                    EARL
               (Washing his hand)
          Hay, all you need in this life is a good
          beer and a good woman.

                    HAY
               (Finishing his beer; Getting up)
          Well I'm going to let you have both I'm
          about to leave.

                    RUTH
          You not gonna stay for dinner?

              HAY
Nah, I just wanted to see how far this fool
was going to go with all of this land talk.

              EARL
You dont know nothing Hay. Henry made a
million down there.

              HAY
A million?! Shid I need to come down and
mess with yall then.

              EARL
Come on then it's alotta land down there.

              RUTH
I don't trust him. He got all those people
workin for him and he be paying them next
to nothing.

              EARL
We family though, that's blood we talkin
bout.

              RUTH
And how is Randy doing?

              HAY
You're little brother is down there too?

              EARL
Yeah he been there for a year now.

              RUTH
How is he doing Earl?

              EARL
Shid I ont know. I ain talk to the nigga in
awhile.

              RUTH

All I'm saying is if he blood and he done
made a million then the least he could do
is help out.

                    EARL
He aint jus gonna give it to me. I gotta
work for it.

                    RUTH
But that's suppose to be blood right?

                    HAY
     (Sensing the tension)
Well I'm going to get up out of here.

                    EARL
You don't want another beer, it's plenty in
there.

                    HAY
Ones plenty for me.

Hay gets up from the table and gives Earl some dap.

                    HAY
Goodnight Ruth.

                    RUTH
Night Hay.

Hay exits, Earl downs his beer and walks to the
fridge for another. He sits back down, scoots his
chair up and reaches for the food.

                    RUTH
Wait for the kids.

                    EARL
Where they at?

                    RUTH
Washing up.

                    EARL
              (Yelling in the kids direction)
         Y'all come on now.

Earl, impatient, gets up, walks over to the counter
and grabs two pieces of bread and sits back down in
his seat.

She looks at him while he eats the bread.

                    RUTH
         What happened at wor-

                    EARL
              (To the kids)
         Y'all come on.

                    RUTH
         What happened at work?

                    EARL
         Nothin.

                    RUTH
         I heard you. What do you mean he not trying
         to pay you.

                    EARL
              (Stern)
         Leave it.

                    RUTH
         Earl stop-

Before she can finish her thought the kids come
running in and settle into their seats. They
recognize the tension between their parents.

They hold hands and say grace after which they all
dig in.

No conversation, they eat in silence all of them defeated by the weight of the day.

INT. FAMILY HOUSE - LIVING ROOM - DAY

MICHELLE sits on the couch watching TV, JUNIOR walks out of the back room fully dressed.

                    MICHELLE
               (Taking notice)
          Where you going?

                    JUNIOR
          Outside.

                    MICHELLE
          Nobody is going to play with you.

                    JUNIOR
          Shut up.

                    MICHELLE
          What you just say to me?

                    JUNIOR
          You don't know what you're talking about.

                    MICHELLE
          Ok have it your way.

He walks towards his mother who is in the kitchen talking on the phone.

                    JUNIOR
          Excuse me ma, do you have any money in case
          the ice cream truck comes?

                    RUTH
          Look in my purse.

                    MICHELLE

That's not fair you don't ever give me money.

JUNIOR taunts MICHELLE.

                    RUTH
I only have a 5. Bring my change back.

                    JUNIOR
THANK YOU!!

He takes the money and walks to the door showing it off to MICHELLE

                    RUTH
Bring your sister back something.

MICHELLE laughs at him, he opens the door and walks out. MICHELLE puts her attention back to the TV.

EXT. SAVANNAH ST. PLAYGROUND - CONTINUOUS

A loose spiral football is soaring through the air landing in the hands of a child who runs, zig zagging his way through a group of boys.

They all gang up on him, and pile on top of him. He gets up and tosses the ball in the air and the whole process starts over.

JUNIOR sits on the swing looking at the various groups of children playing, deciding which group he wants to be a part of. He notices the boys playing football, laughing, dapping each other up. He takes a deep breath and walks over to the boys.

                    JUNIOR
Can I play?

                    BOY 1
Yeah that's cool with me.

                    JUNIOR
          How I play?

All the boys standing around start to laugh.

                    BOY 1
          It's simple. Catch the ball, run to that
          pole right there and try not to get
          tackled.

                    JUNIOR
          That's it?

                    BOY 1
          That's it.

He reaches his hand out to give JUNIOR a pound. He
looks on in shock at first then quickly pounds the
boy's fist.

                    BOY 1
          Y'all ready?

They all say yes.

                    BOY 1
              (To JUNIOR)
          You ready?

JUNIOR gives a thumbs up. The boy looks back at all
the other boys, they look back at him smirking. They
all have malicious intent.

He tosses the ball in the air, and JUNIOR catches
it, quickly taking off. He's doing good avoiding
tackles, he's quick and agile, he almost reaches the
other end until...

A boy lands a big hit on JUNIOR slamming him to the
ground. All of the kids around him get hype, JUNIOR
gets up and goes straight towards the boy.

                    JUNIOR
          What the hell was that?

                    BOY 2
          Just throw the ball up.

He pauses, looking at the first boy who encouraged
him to play, not say anything, smiling, finding
humor in the pain being caused.

                  BOY 3 (O.S.)
             THROW THE DAMN BALL.

JUNIOR slams the ball to the ground and runs off.
The kids don't chase, but their insults towards
JUNIOR are just as fast.

He runs deep into the woods still trying to outrun
the humiliation, he stops and looks back. The
laughter is no longer heard.

He closes his eyes and uses his senses to escape.

He feels the breeze between his fingers, the same
breeze that causes the leaves and branches to dance
during this heat filled day. He moves his feet
feeling the sticks underneath him, slowly moving
them to become one with the ground.

He hears the cicadas that roar in the trees and
suddenly quiet down. He hears the birds
communicating with each other through song.

His escape is suddenly hindered by the overwhelming
sound of a fly. He swats it away but it persists,
more flies begin to be heard. He opens his eyes, now
sniffing as well.

This smell, a foul stench, that isn't lost or new to
those who often find themselves in the woods. Like a
dog he follows the smell. It leads him even deeper
into the woods.

CLOSE UP ON:

A body decomposing in the tall grass, flies
surrounding it. The damage, two gunshot wounds, one
to the head and another to the chest. His hair in a
temp fade, his clothes are relatively new, his shoes
the only thing missing. He was dumped here,
abandoned.

JUNIOR looks at this boy indifferently, and
shockingly with no fear. However, another emotion
begins to rise as he looks over this body...

ENVY.

Music from an ice cream truck rings in the distance,
JUNIOR walks off, leaving the body to rest.

                                            CUT TO:

EXT. SAVANNAH ST. - CONTINUOUS

An ice cream truck cruising down the street playing
its classic jingle.

Kids are coming from every direction chasing behind
this truck, some on bikes but primarily on foot.

The truck comes to a stop at the end of the block
and the kids crowd around it. A black man opens the
door, everyone knows him and he knows the kids.

                    ICE CREAM MAN
          Uh-Uh line up like y'all got some sense.
          Y'all parents taught y'all better than that
          come on line it up.

The kids line up.

                    ICE CREAM MAN
          What you want?

                    GIRL 1
          How much the fruities?

                    ICE CREAM MAN
          Girl you've been coming to this truck all
          summer, they a dolla, a dolla a bag.

                    GIRL 1
          Gimme two of em.

                    ICE CREAM MAN
          GIMME?

                    GIRL 1
                  (Attitude)
          Can I have two of them please?

                    ICE CREAM MAN
          Yes ma'am.

He takes the money and gives her the fruities.

                    ICE CREAM MAN
          NEXT!

                    GIRL 2
          Can I have a pickle egg and some sunflower
          seeds?

                    ICE CREAM MAN
          You gonna add some mints to that too right?

                                             CUT TO:

EXT. SAVANNAH ST. - CONTINUOUS

JUNIOR walks toward the truck, the same boys who he
had played football with him earlier approach him.

                    BOY 1
          Aye Junior buy me something from the truck.

                    BOY 2
          Me too.

                    JUNIOR
          No.

                    BOY 1
          Is this because of the game? Come on man
          it's just football.

                    JUNIOR
          I said no.

One of the boys get in front of him.

                    BOY 1
          I don't remember asking.

JUNIOR tries to run through the boys but he can't.
They grab him and start going through his pockets.
They find a five dollar bill.

                    BOY 1
          See I knew you were holding out.

JUNIOR gets up and pushes him.

                    JUNIOR
          Give it back.

The boy walks up to JUNIOR and punches him in the
stomach. JUNIOR falls to the ground.

They all walk off laughing, JUNIOR gets up slowly,
looking at the boys leave with his money.

INT. FAMILY HOUSE - LIVING ROOM - CONTINUOUS

JUNIOR burst through the door, MICHELLE is still on
the couch, their mother on the phone.

                    MICHELLE

What happened to you?

He gets to his mother.

> JUNIOR
> Mom that boy took my money.

> RUTH
> (To the phone)
> I'm gonna call you back.

She hangs up the phone.

> RUTH
> You mean he took *MY* money.

> MICHELLE (O.S.)
> I told you not to go outside.

> JUNIOR
> Shut up Michelle. This is none of your business.

> RUTH
> It is now. Go back out there with your brother and find that boy.

> MICHELLE
> What?

> JUNIOR
> You can't be serious. It's just five dollars.

> RUTH
> That's my five dollars, boy go out there and get my damn money back.

JUNIOR walks over to the couch sitting down, MICHELLE goes and puts on her shoes tying them up tight and putting her hair back.

MICHELLE is at the door now.

                    MICHELLE
                  (To JUNIOR)
            Come on.

He gets up and goes to the door, he looks back at
his mom, not saying a word those eyes alone, showing
fear, begging his mother not to let him go.

She picks up the phone and dials another number.
JUNIOR looks back while MICHELLE shuts the door
behind them.

EXT. SAVANNAH ST. - CONTINUOUS

MICHELLE and JUNIOR are walking down the street.

                    MICHELLE
            Why didn't you do anything when he first
            took it?

                    JUNIOR
            It was three of them.

                    MICHELLE
            That's why I'm here to make sure it's a
            fair fight.

JUNIOR stops.

                    JUNIOR
            I don't want to fight.

MICHELLE stops taking a deep breath. She turns
around and walks up to JUNIOR.

                    MICHELLE
            Why don't you stand up for yourself? You
            gonna just let someone beat you, take your
            shit and get away with it? No, that's not
            happening. Stop letting these people think
            you weak.

MICHELLE turns to walk away. JUNIOR remains there.

                    MICHELLE (O.S.)
          LETS GO.

JUNIOR slowly follows behind.

EXT. SAVANNAH ST. PLAYGROUND - CONTINUOUS

JAVON, his two friends, and other neighborhood kids
are sitting around eating their snacks.

                    MICHELLE
          HEY!

They all look up.

                    MICHELLE
          You think you can just take my brothers
          shit and jump him, you that much of a punk
          that you can't fight him one on one.

                    JAVON
          Alright lets go then what's up.

All the kids start to circle around JUNIOR and
JAVON, shouting and screaming coming from all
directions.

JAVON gets into his stance, he walks toward JUNIOR
whose hands are down. He looks at MICHELLE.

                    MICHELLE
          Come on.

JUNIOR turns his head and JAVON fires off multiple
punches to JUNIOR'S face and body. He pushes him
down to the ground.

                    JAVON
          Get up.

JUNIOR looks at his sister wanting her to help, but can't knowing that it is a one on one fight.

He looks up at JAVON who is still in a fighting stance, without hesitation he runs out the circle and back into the woods.

All the other kids laugh as a boy walks up to MICHELLE.

                    BOY 1
          Your brother is a bitch.

                    MICHELLE
          Shut the hell up, you would've got whooped
          too.

The kids slowly disperse, MICHELLE looks in the direction of the woods, her brother vanishing.

                                        CUT TO:

EXT. SAVANNAH ST. - WOODS - CONTINUOUS
JUNIOR'S eyes looking at us, innocent and ashamed. Tears begin forming in his eyes, one escapes and falls down his cheek. He quickly catches it but he can't catch them all as they begin to stream down his face.

He begins to breathe angrily, that shame fueling a hate filled rage that's been begging to come out. He snaps letting out a savage scream as he viciously beats the tree with a stick.

He grunts with each hit, the tears falling down his cheeks make him even more angry, his hands bleeding from the tight grip he has on the stick, his sounds become more animalistic than human with every blow.

The cat from earlier walks up to JUNIOR staying at a distance, he watches him in this state. JUNIOR feels the cat's presence, he turns around and lets out an angry and enraged scream towards the cat who scurries off.

JUNIOR falls to his knees, crying.

                    JUNIOR
          Don't go.

INT. FAMILY HOUSE - LIVING ROOM

JUNIOR opens the door of the apartment.

CLOSE UP ON:

The belt in their mother's hand.

MICHELLE sits on the couch, her eyes red from crying. She's already gotten her whooping.

She gets up and walks over to him growing in size with each step.

Silence, then...

                    RUTH
               (A calm seriousness)
          I don't whoop clothes.

JUNIOR turns around and drops his pants. His mother whoops him. We don't see it, but we can hear JUNIORS cries as we focus on MICHELLE'S face, not looking and crying at the sound of her brother in pain.

INT. KIDS BEDROOM - NIGHT

MICHELLE and JUNIOR are facing each other. She's asleep but JUNIOR is wide awake. Something clearly on his mind.

                    JUNIOR
                  (Whispering)
              Michelle. Michelle.

MICHELLE rolls over, putting her back towards him.

                    JUNIOR
          I'm sorry Michelle. I'm sorry.

He rolls over, their backs now facing each other,
laying in a fractured togetherness, *distant* in the
same bed as we...

                                        FADE TO BLACK.

                END OF ACT I: SUMMER
Over BLACK, Just The Two Of Us by Bill Withers plays
through a radio. We also begin to hear water
sloshing around and a woman humming to the song.

                                        FADE IN:

INT. FAMILY HOUSE - MORNING

An iron gliding on two sets of uniform clothes.
Their mother breezes through each article of
clothing.

She looks at the time...

...7:45 AM

She finishes up the clothes, and carries them down
the hall. The bathroom door is open and JUNIOR is
standing in the mirror brushing his teeth.

                    RUTH
              She up yet?

JUNIOR shrugs. She looks in the direction of the
door and marches towards it.

INT. KIDS BEDROOM - CONTINUOUS

MICHELLE is knocked out sleep, comfortable, drool
falling down her cheek.

Her mother comes through the door.

                    RUTH
          GET UP!! It's almost 8.

MICHELLE turns around slowly and opens her eyes,
mentally in a whole other world. She places the
clothes on the bed.

                    RUTH
          If I come back in here and you still sleep
          we are gonna have a problem.

She walks out and JUNIOR comes in preparing to get
dressed.

                    MICHELLE
          So you wasn't going to wake me up.

JUNIOR doesn't say anything, he continues getting
dressed.

                    MICHELLE
          Ok. Remember that.

She storms out of the bed and out of the room.

INT. FAMILY HOUSE - FRONT DOOR - CONTINUOUS

Their mom rubs Vaseline on their faces, both kids
complain while moving their heads around. She
reaches in her pockets and pulls out some lunch
money.

She hands it to MICHELLE.

                    JUNIOR

I can hold my own money.

She opens the door.

                    RUTH
          Go on before y'all be late, and zip up
          those jackets.

They both start to head out the door.

                    RUTH
          Wait Junior I almost forgot.

She runs off, and returns with a small sketchbook in
hand.

                    RUTH
          Here, I got it yesterday.

                    JUNIOR
          Thank you.

She pulls him closer.

                    RUTH
          You be a man ok. I don't care what happens
          be a man today.

He looks at her, and although she is looking back at
him he still feels unseen. He walks out of the door.

                    MICHELLE (O.S.)
          Hurry up Junior.

JUNIOR does a slight jog catching up to her. More
kids from the neighborhood join in.

                    MICHELLE
          What did mom want?

                    JUNIOR
          She was just giving me that sketchbook I
          asked for.

                    MICHELLE
          It ain't like you can draw or anything.

JUNIOR looks at her, shaking his head at the
comment. They continue their walk as other kids from
the neighborhood join them and they all talk to
MICHELLE pushing JUNIOR further away, now on the
outside of the group.

INT. JOHN THOMAS MIDDLE SCHOOL - CLASSROOM - DAY

A classroom in slight chaos, nobody is up moving
around but the students are clearly not paying
attention to the teacher.

The teacher could care less if they paid attention
or not.

                    MR. ROWE
                 (Unenthused)
          In two weeks, you will be performing your
          monologues to the class. I have printed out
          monologues for you to use. They must be
          memorized.

The teacher continues to introduce the assignment,
we see JUNIOR doodling in the sketchbook. While
everyone has someone to sit with, JUNIOR is alone.

A girl behind him reaches forward, dropping a note
over his shoulder.

He looks back at the girl, her head down.

He opens the note and reads it. He looks at the back
of the classroom noticing a group of boys laughing
at him.

He crumbles up the note and goes back to doodling.

Suddenly...

A paper ball hits him in the head.

He ignores it and then another is thrown, hitting him in the head again. He gets up and heads to the door.

                    MR. ROWE
          Excuse me, where are you going?

                    JUNIOR
             (In stride)
          To the bathroom.

                    MR. ROWE
          No, go back to your seat.

                    JUNIOR
          No.

                    MR. ROWE
          Who do you think you're talking to?

                    JUNIOR
             (Voice raising)
          You don't see what they're doing back
          there.

                    MR. ROWE
          I see you right now. Go to your seat.

                    JUNIOR
             (Pleading)
          Mr. Rowe.

                    MR. ROWE
          TO YOUR SEAT!!!

The kids in the classroom all laugh, JUNIOR walks back to his seat and puts his head down.

The teacher goes back to delivering the assignment.

Another note is pass to him, he opens, it reads:

"I'M FINNA FUK U UP BITCH"

He crumbles up the paper and puts his head down. Paper balls continuing to fling his way as the teacher turns around to write something on the board.

A woman knocks at the door and enters.

                    GUIDANCE COUNSELOR
          Good Morning class, Mr. Rowe can I see you
          real quick.

Mr. Rowe heads to the door and the class erupts in chatter.

The teacher comes back with a girl, black, pretty and with a beautiful smile.

The teacher places a hand on the girl's shoulders.

                    MR. ROWE
          Class, this is our new student Penny.
          Please give her a special John Thomas
          welcome.

The class doesn't say anything, everyone is just staring at her, head to toe judging. JUNIOR looks at her, his eyes wide, she glances back at him and smiles. Unlike JUNIOR, her eyes are filled with life and joy. He quickly looks down, continuing to draw.

                    MR. ROWE
          You can take that seat over there.

She walks over to JUNIOR, and takes her seat. They don't say anything to each other. JUNIOR keeps drawing, fighting the urge to look at her.

INT. JOHN THOMAS MIDDLE SCHOOL - CAFETERIA - CONTINUOUS

JUNIOR sits at a table by himself, eating his food, and people watching. MICHELLE sits across the cafeteria with a group of people, a boy sitting beside her tries to touch her thigh, she pushes it away slowly but the boy is persistent.

JUNIOR feels his sister's discomfort but not knowing how to approach it. He shakes his head, pushing his food away and doodles in his notebook.

We hear a soft voice.

                    VOICE (O.S.)
          Can I sit here?

He looks up and sees that it is PENNY. He is taken aback, silent.

                    PENNY
          Well can I?

He nods his head and PENNY sits in front of him. He's uncomfortable not use to someone being in front of him during this time of day.

                    PENNY
          You don't talk much do you?

JUNIOR doesn't look up at her.

                    PENNY
          Can I least know your name?

His eyes glued to the notebook. PENNY sits back and studies him.

                    PENNY
          Well I know you're not deaf. Maybe you
          speak French or something.

PENNY tries to say something in French but it is obviously terrible. JUNIOR chuckles.

                    PENNY
          So HE IS FRENCH. Who would've thought a
          french boy in DC.

                    SECURITY (O.S.)
          Lunch will be over in 10 minutes, start
          throwing your trash away.

JUNIOR is still doodling, PENNNY eyes JUNIOR'S
barely eaten lunch tray. JUNIOR glances at her,
seeing her looking at the food.

                    JUNIOR
          You hungry?

                    PENNY
          And he speaks English too.

                    JUNIOR
          I see you looking, do you want some.
               (Sliding the tray over)
          I just want the milk you can have
          everything else. I'm not hungry.

                    PENNY
               (Pause)
          You sure?

He nods his head and starts back doodling. PENNY
starts to eat, devouring this food.

                    PENNY
          What's your name little French Boy?

                    JUNIOR
          Earl; but everyone calls me Junior

                    PENNY
          Damn you gotta old ass name.

                    JUNIOR
               (Serious)

Are you joaning?

                    PENNY
No, I just never met someone our age with a
name so old. What's your last name?

                    JUNIOR
You the police or something?

                    PENNY
Maybe I am.

                    JUNIOR
I don't trust cops.

                    PENNY
You can trust me.

                    JUNIOR
Why?

She points at her skin.

                    JUNIOR
Nope; definitely not happening.

She lets out a laugh that turns peoples heads, it's
loud, unique, and a bit infectious. She doesn't even
try to hold it in.

                                        CUT TO:
MICHELLE looks at her brother and Penny laughing.

                    MICHELLE
Who is that?

RANAE looks back.

                    BOY 1
That's Penny, she looks good too.

                    RANAE
Why she eating your brother food?

                    MICHELLE
              (Getting up)
     I don't know but I'm about to find out.

A group of boys walk up to JUNIOR. One of the boys
grabs JUNIORS's milk.

                    BOY 1
          You ain't gonna mind right? Ain't like you
          drinking it.

Another boy peaks over and grabs JUNIOR'S journal,
tossing it around.

                    BOY 2
          Aye CJ catch.

CJ catches the journal and starts ripping pages from
it.

                    JUNIOR
          LEAVE ME ALONE.

                    CJ
          Or what?!

MICHELLE pushes CJ.

                    MICHELLE
          He said leave him alone.

                    CJ
          I'd beat the shit out of you and your
          brother.

                    MICHELLE
          Do it then.

The cafeteria starts to get loud, everyone looks in
their direction.

                    SECURITY
              (Getting between everyone)

What's the problem?

                    MICHELLE
               (Staring CJ down)
          It ain't no problem, right?

                    CJ
          We was just playin.

                    SECURITY
          Then y'all sit down then. Matter of fact.
          EVERYONE LUNCH IS OVER LETS LINE IT UP.

The boys walk off, CJ bumps into JUNIOR.

                    CJ
               (To JUNIOR)
          Bitch.

JUNIOR bends down to pick up the torn pages from the
journal. PENNY tries to help.

                    MICHELLE
               (To Penny)
          He's fine. I got him, you can leave.

PENNY gets up and leaves.

                    MICHELLE
               (To Penny)
          And don't eat my brother's food again.

MICHELLE helps him pick up the remaining pages.
Tears begin forming in JUNIOR's eyes.

                    MICHELLE
               (Looking around at everyone)
          Nope, not here. Either hold it in or go to
          the bathroom. Don't let these people see
          you cry.

JUNIOR gets up, grabs the journal and walks out with the other kids.

INT. JOHN THOMAS MIDDLE SCHOOL - BATHROOM - CONTINUOUS

JUNIOR washes his face off in the sink, he looks up at the mirror, his eyes red and nose stuffy.

He breathes deeply, nice and slow. His eyes close, and his hands grab the sink firmly. Similar to the woods, he tries to escape his world, wanting to be anywhere but here.

The bell rings, chatter and footsteps can be heard from outside the bathroom door, he opens his eyes, defeated, he's still here.

INT. TIGER MART - DAY

The school day has ended, MICHELLE, JUNIOR and RANAE are in their local corner store.

>   MICHELLE
>   Why was that girl eating your food?

>   JUNIOR
>   She was hungry.

>   RANAE
>   She wasn't hungry I saw her eat before she
>   ate your food.

>   JUNIOR
>   That isn't true.

MICHELLE pulls out a couple dollar bills from her pocket.

>   JUNIOR
>   Where'd you get that?

                    MICHELLE
          What do you think?

                    JUNIOR
          Why aren't you eating?

                    MICHELLE
          I could say the same thing to you.

MICHELLE grabs some candy and goes to the register.

                    JUNIOR
          You always get sick when you eat candy
          before dinner.

                    MICHELLE
          Please, shut up.

                    RANAE
          Can you get me something?

                    MICHELLE
          You don't ever have no money. Go get one
          thing. I'm serious I'm not getting you two
          things.

RANAE walks off to grab candy.

                    JUNIOR
          You need to start eating.

                    MICHELLE
          Just worry about yourself.

                    JUNIOR
          Why are you acting like that? I'm just
          trying to help.

                    MICHELLE
          You can't even help yourself.

                    JUNIOR
          (Under his breath)

That's why I don't like you.

                    MICHELLE
What?

                    JUNIOR
That's why I don't like you.

                    MICHELLE
And nobody likes you so I guess we're even.

He's had enough, he storms out of the Tiger Mart and
walks down the street.

RANAE comes back with her one piece of candy.
MICHELLE pays and they walk out the store.

INT. KIDS BEDROOM - NIGHT

MICHELLE is asleep, JUNIOR lays on his back looking
at the ceiling, he doesn't sleep much, his mind in
constant thought.

MICHELLE jumps up, vomiting everywhere. She holds
her mouth and sprints to the bathroom.

INT. BATHROOM - CONTINUOUS

JUNIOR follows her, creeping up to the door and
watches her throw up in the toilet.

Their mother rushes into the bathroom, tending to
MICHELLE.

                    RUTH
She throw up in the room?

                    JUNIOR
Yes.

                    RUTH

> Go get that cleaning stuff from under the
> sink.

JUNIOR walks off, we hear him opening and shutting a
cabinet.

He walks back into the frame as MICHELLE continues
to vomit.

INT. KIDS BEDROOM - CONTINUOUS

JUNIOR turns on the lights, seeing the spots where
MICHELLE puked. He gets on his hands and knees and
begins cleaning it.

                                              CUT TO:

INT. KIDS BEDROOM - THE NEXT MORNING

JUNIOR is alone in bed, wide awake, eyeing the
clock, watching it as it strikes 7 AM. The alarm
sounds off.

He doesn't turn it off right away, he sits with the
sound.

INT. PARENTS ROOM - CONTINUOUS

JUNIOR is standing in the doorway of his parents'
bedroom. He's unfamiliar to this room only entering
when it is absolutely necessary.

MICHELLE is laying down in bed as JUNIOR walks up to
her.

                    JUNIOR
                 (Tapping)
              Michelle.

She opens her eyes.

                    JUNIOR
          You going to school today?

                   MICHELLE
          What does it look like?

                    JUNIOR
          Are you that sick?

MICHELLE ignores him.

                    JUNIOR
              (Fearful, Whispering)
          Come on Michelle you have to go.

Their mom comes into the room.

                     RUTH
          Get dressed before you be late.

                    JUNIOR
                 (Whispering)
          Michelle.

                   MICHELLE
          I don't feel good.

JUNIOR slowly walks out of the room.

INT. FRONT DOOR - CONTINUOUS

His mother stands in front of him as he zips up his
jacket. She licks her finger and wipes some dried up
crust from his eye.

                     RUTH
          You'll be alright.

JUNIOR looks up at her, there is an uncertainty in
that line that they both feel but don't want to
admit.

She gives him a kiss and she opens the door, he walks out and heads down the street.

INT. JOHN THOMAS MIDDLE SCHOOL - HALLWAY - DAY

JUNIOR is putting the stuff from his backpack into his locker. He looks down the hall and sees CJ and his followers laughing at him. He doesn't pay them any mind.

The bell rings. He looks down the hall and sees that his classroom door is closing.

                    JUNIOR
          Wait Ms.Lewis.

He slams the locker and jogs to class.

A girl sticks out her foot, tripping him up. His papers and books flying everywhere he looks to see who did it but everyone has dispersed into their classrooms.

He roams the halls, skipping, trying to avoid faculty and security guards. He hears a walkie talkie from down the hall. He has nowhere to go, but the girls restroom. The sound gets closer, and he ducks in cover behind the door.

The sound passes and as he prepares to leave, he hears someone crying from the back stall. He moves deeper into the bathroom closer to the crying. He looks down at the shoes recognizing them instantly.

                    JUNIOR
          Penny?

                    PENNY
          Who is that?

                    JUNIOR

It's Junior.

                    PENNY
          What are you doing in here?

                    JUNIOR
          Why are you crying?

                    PENNY
          Just go.

                    JUNIOR
          Penny I just want to-

                    PENNY
          LEAVE before I tell someone you're in here.

JUNIOR starts walking towards the door.

                    PENNY
          Wait.

The stall door opens. She slowly walks out of the stall, turning around and revealing a blood stain on the back of her pants.

                    PENNY
          I can't go out there like this. Everyone will think I'm disgusting.

PENNY starts to cry again. JUNIOR, takes off his jacket and extends his arm.

                    JUNIOR
          Take this.

PENNY looks up.

                    JUNIOR
          Wrap it around your waist. The nurse should be able to help you.

She takes the jacket and wraps it around her waist.

                    PENNY
          You're not freaked out?

                    JUNIOR
          Not at all.

Another walkie talkie is heard outside the door.

                    JUNIOR
          Ima get out of here.

He turns to leave.

                    PENNY
          Junior.

He turns around.

                    PENNY
          Thank you.

                    JUNIOR
          I got you.

JUNIOR smiles, he looks both ways and walks out.

INT. JOHN THOMAS MIDDLE SCHOOL - HALLWAY

The final bell rings. JUNIOR moves through a sea of
children opening up their lockers and talking to
each other.

He looks down the hall and sees PENNY smiling, his
jacket around her waist she signals for him to come
to her. He takes a few steps but stops.

Behind PENNY is CJ and his followers. He walks in
the opposite direction, they follow behind him. He
moves quickly through the dismissal traffic trying
not to run.

EXT. JOHN THOMAS MIDDLE SCHOOL - SCHOOL YARD - DAY

JUNIOR opens the door and keeps walking with the boys closing in on him. This walking turns into a jog which then leads to a sprint and the boys follow suit.

The chase is on, and it closely resembles a wildlife hunt.

In a panic JUNIOR runs across a busy street, dodging a car that brakes just in time.

He continues running and bursts through the doors of an…

INT/EXT. APARTMENT BUILDING - DAY - CONTINUOUS

An apartment complex. A flickering dim light illuminating each part of the building. JUNIOR continues running through the halls, picking up his speed just enough so that he can duck behind a doorway.

The boys run past, their footsteps getting further away. JUNIOR leaves his hiding spot and walks with caution through this hell hole of a place. A rat darts across his feet causing him to shriek and run.

He sees a door that leads outside and he runs straight towards it at full speed bursting through it.

EXT. BACKSIDE OF THE APARTMENT COMPLEX - CONTINUOUS

A group of older boys and girls jump, startled by the door being forced open.

A boy caught off guard has pulled a gun out on JUNIOR. He stares into the barrel, breathes deep, and closes his eyes. Unfazed, ready to die.

BOY 1

Jerrod put that away before you hurt
somebody.

He puts the gun away.

                    JERROD

               (To Junior)
          You can't just be running up on people like
          that. You're gonna mess around and get
          killed doing shit like that.

JUNIOR looks over, and sees the boys that were
chasing him, still on the prowl. He moves away
hiding himself behind the much taller JERROD.

                    BOY 1 (O.S.)
          You look scared as hell.

                    GIRL 1
          What you think he just had a gun in his
          face

JERROD notices JUNIOR hiding, he follows his eyes
and sees the boys in the distance.

                    JERROD
          They was chasin you?

JUNIOR nods his head.

                    JERROD
          You can't run forever shorty.

JUNIOR watches the boys in the distance, beginning
to walk away disappearing from view.

EXT. SAVANNAH TERRANCE - EVENING

The sun is beginning to set while JUNIOR walks down
the street getting closer to his neighborhood.

                    PENNY (O.S.)
          You know it's dangerous to be walking
          around here by yourself.

JUNIOR stops, that voice never fails to put a smile
on his face. He turns to face her.

                    PENNY
          Where you coming from?

                    JUNIOR
          I was just walking.

                    PENNY
          With those boys that was running after you?

                    JUNIOR
          Nah; I wasn't-

                    PENNY
          You don't have to lie to me Junior. I
          really don't like liars.

He looks around.

                    JUNIOR
          Your mom home?

                    PENNY
          No.

                    JUNIOR
          Will she be back anytime soon?

                    PENNY
          No.

A beat from JUNIOR, a thought weighs heavy on his
mind.

                    PENNY
          What's up?

                    JUNIOR
                 (Walking closer)
       I really don't want to go home right now.

They both stare at each other.

INT. PENNY'S HOUSE - CONTINUOUS

An apartment similar to JUNIOR'S however, it lacks
the necessary items that would turn it into a home.
No pictures or artwork, just essential appliances.

                    JUNIOR
                 (Looking around)
           Where's your mom?

                    PENNY (O.S.)
           I don't know.

There is a stack of past due notices on the table
that JUNIOR notices.

                    PENNY (O.S.)
           Do you want some water? I'd offer food but
           I just ate the rest of the noodles.

                    JUNIOR
           Water's cool.

PENNY grabs a glass from the cabinet and fills it
with tap water. She walks over to JUNIOR handing him
the glass, she takes the past due envelopes and puts
them in a drawer. He takes a sip from the water and
notices a large, clunky desktop computer in the
corner.

                    JUNIOR
           What were you doing over there?

                    PENNY

Finding my monologue to perform for Mr.
Rowe's class.

                    JUNIOR
You're actually doing that?

                    PENNY
It's a grade.

JUNIOR takes another sip from his water.

                    JUNIOR
What monologue are you doing?

                    PENNY
Rose from Fences. The "I was standing with
you" one.

                    JUNIOR
I have no idea what you're talking about.

                    PENNY
          (Deep breath)
You've never heard of Fences?

JUNIOR shakes his head. PENNY grabs his hand and
walks over to the computer, showing him the screen.

                    PENNY
You've really never heard of this?

                    JUNIOR
Nope.

                    PENNY
Junior if we're going to be friends then
you have to learn this stuff.

A slight hesitation.

                    JUNIOR
Friends?

                    PENNY
          Yeah.

Silence from JUNIOR.

                    PENNY
          What, you've never had a friend before?

He finishes his drink, his silence answers her
question.

                    PENNY
          Can you at least sit down? I don't like
          people standing up over me.

She scoots over in her chair, he sits down. They
continue watching the movie. PENNY'S eyes are glued
to the screen in awe of Viola Davis's performance.

                    JUNIOR
          You must really like acting.

                    PENNY
          That's what I want to do when I get older.
          Ima be in all the movies, magazine covers,
          all of that.

                    JUNIOR
          Are you any good at it?

                    PENNY
          We all are.

                    JUNIOR
          No I'm not.

                    PENNY
          We're all actors JUNIOR. Everyday we
          pretend to be someone else to protect
          ourselves.

                    JUNIOR

Where you learn that at?

                    PENNY
          You really need to start paying attention
          in class.

They both laugh.

                    JUNIOR
          I guess I'm not good at it. My acting
          skills ain't protect me yet.

PENNY turns her head to look at him, although he
isn't serious there's a truth within those words.

                    PENNY
          I'll teach you. I'll help you with your
          monologue.

JUNIOR looks at her and for the first time he feels
seen. He smiles at her speechless.

                    PENNY
          Now we just need to find you a monologue.
          To save time we can just use one from the
          same play.

                    JUNIOR
          I don't know Penny.

                    PENNY
          Come on Junior. I got you.

We pull back watching PENNY help JUNIOR, their
voices, free of worry, focused on the moment,
enjoying each other.

                                        CUT TO:

INT. KIDS BEDROOM - NIGHT

MICHELLE is lying down in bed, while JUNIOR puts on
lotion.

                    MICHELLE
          Why did it take you so long to get home?

                    JUNIOR
          I stayed after for tutoring.

MICHELLE looks at him.

                    MICHELLE
          You're just gonna sit there and lie to me
          like that.

                    JUNIOR
          I'm not I had tutoring and I took the long
          way home.

                    MICHELLE
          Is that where you lost your jacket?

JUNIOR is silent, he didn't think anybody noticed.

                    MICHELLE
          Who has your jacket? CJ?

                    JUNIOR
               (Pause)
          Penny.

MICHELLE sucks her teeth.

                    JUNIOR
          She needed it.

                    MICHELLE
          For what? She wanted to see how good you
          smell?

                    JUNIOR
               (Getting in the bed)
          You don't know what you're talking about.

                    MICHELLE
          Don't say I didn't warn you. I've been
          right every time when it comes to you.

MICHELLE plops herself back down. JUNIOR lays down
contemplating, maybe she is right.

INT. JOHN THOMAS MIDDLE SCHOOL - CLASSROOM - DAY

A half-ass round of applause is given as PENNY walks
back to her seat.

                    MR. ROWE
          Fantastic job, that was beautiful.

JUNIOR fist bumps her as she sits.

                    MR. ROWE
          Lastly we have Earl.

Some kids start to laugh.

                    MR. ROWE
          If you didn't come up here you got no
          business laughing.

                    PENNY
              (To JUNIOR, in a whisper)
          You got this.

He gets up and walks to the front of the class. All
eyes are on him. It isn't unfamiliar, it's just for
a different purpose.

                    MR. ROWE
              (To Earl)
          What monologue are you doing?

                    JUNIOR
          My name is Earl. I'll be doing a monologue
          from August Wilsons' *Fences*.

He begins the "I don't have to like you" monologue
from *Fences*. He starts off strong, channeling his
inner Denzel, copying his mannerisms all while
putting his own youthful touch to the words.

He stumbles on a word, and he pauses. He closes his
eyes to think, trying to remember the line. He looks
at PENNY as she's trying to mouth the words but he
can't follow. All of his momentum is lost.

> JUNIOR
> (To Mr. Rowe)
> Sorry.

He walks back to his seat.

> MR. ROWE
> Students please make sure that you have the
> lines for these monologues memorized.

EXT. JOHN THOMAS MIDDLE SCHOOL - SCHOOL YARD - DAY

The school day has ended.

JUNIOR is walking fast out of the door. PENNY is
close behind him.

> PENNY
> Junior.

He keeps walking.

> PENNY
> Junior wait up.

She catches up to him.

> PENNY
> What's wrong?

> JUNIOR
> That was embarrassing.

                    PENNY
          No it wasn't you were good.

He stops, turning to her.

                    JUNIOR
          Just leave me alone. I don't need any
          friends.

He walks away, and she follows behind him.

                    PENNY
          I'm not giving up on you. That's not what
          friends do. I'm here to help you. You
          helped me now let me help you.

JUNIOR stops. PENNY looks off and sees a metrobus
pulling up.

                    PENNY
          Come with me somewhere?

                    JUNIOR
          What about your mom?

                    PENNY
          She doesn't care. Come on.

She grabs his hand and they run off.

MICHELLE walks out of the school building, RANAE
beside her.

                    RANAE
               (Pointing)
          Look.

MICHELLE turns her head and sees her brother running
on the bus.

                    RANAE
          You better say something to him.

                    MICHELLE
          He'll learn.

INT. METRO BUS - CONTINUOUS

PENNY and JUNIOR ride on the bus, they look out the
window, turning back to each other, laughing and
talking.

PENNY pulls the yellow chord.

They have reached their destination...

EXT. ANACOSTIA RIVER - CONTINUOUS

PENNY and JUNIOR sit looking at the water both
quiet, taking in the sounds.

                    JUNIOR
          How'd you find this place?

                    PENNY
          Everyone from DC know about Anacostia.

                    JUNIOR
          Nah I mean like how did you find this
          specific spot.

                    PENNY
          I went looking for my mom one day and I got
          lost. I was in the house for days and she
          never came, so I got on a bus and went
          looking for her.

PENNY'S eyes stay on the water, JUNIOR looks at her,
not knowing what to say, realizing that just his
being there is enough.

                    PENNY

>   I saw on the screen Anacostia River I got
>   off, sat right here and just looked at the
>   water.
>   (Pause, then)
>   If you're gonna be alone why not look at
>   something nice.

Silence, both of them looking out into the water.

>   PENNY
>   Oh, I almost forgot.

She reaches into her bag and pulls out his jacket.

>   PENNY
>   I had to wash it at least.

He grabs it from her. She gives him a hug, it's
tight and filled with love, a part of her not
wanting to let go.

>   PENNY
>   Thank you Junior.

JUNIOR hugs her back.

>   JUNIOR
>   Anything for you.

They stare at each other and then at the water,
embracing the silence between them. Together, they
are free of expectations, and of pressure to be
something or someone that they are not. They no
longer have to act. In each other they have found a
home.

INT. METRO BUS - EVENING

The bus cruises through the city. JUNIOR looks at
the streetlights through the window as they grow in
size and then vanish from his peripheral.

PENNY dozing off resting her head on his shoulder as the bus continues its ride back to Savannah St as we...

                              FADE TO BLACK.

<u>END OF ACT II: FALL</u>

INT. PENNY'S HOUSE - DAY

Over darkness we hear...

A ceiling fan whirling at a high speed. Keys jingling, the door opens briefly illuminating the room with light that is coming from the hallway

PENNY and JUNIOR enter.

                    JUNIOR
          You need a thicker coat.

                    PENNY
          You don't see me complaining.

                    JUNIOR
          You should be, it's cold as hell out there.

                    PENNY
          Just turn on that light please.

The sounds of footsteps walking in two different directions. JUNIOR switches the light on and jumps.

                    JUNIOR
          Shit.

                    PENNY (O.S.)
          What?

                    JUNIOR
          Is your mom ok?

                    PENNY (O.S.)
            She sleeps like this all the time.

Items being tossed around in the distance.

                       PENNY
                    (To herself)
            Where is it? I know it's here.

JUNIOR looks over to where the computer once was.

                       JUNIOR
            What happened to the computer?

                       PENNY
            I'm trying to focus Junior, give me a
            second please.

Silence, the only noise coming from PENNY as she
continues looking through the closet.

                       JUNIOR
            What are you looking for?

                       PENNY
            GOT IT.

The door slams, PENNY walks back over to JUNIOR.

                       PENNY
            Let's go.

                       JUNIOR
            Are you kidding me it's cold out there.

                       PENNY
            You'll be alright.

PENNY darts out of the door, and JUNIOR follows
behind her. He shuts the front door but leaves the
light on.

We are still in this room. The mother gives a deathly groan, we hear her shifting her weight on the couch getting in another position.

Her hand plops down, a small crack pipe falls from her hand, rolling against the tile floor.

EXT. ANACOSTIA RIVER (THE SPOT) - CONTINUOUS

We are in the middle of winter. The trees are leafless, and there are blotches of snow that surround them. JUNIOR is sitting looking at the water and PENNY is looking inside the box that she picked up.

                    JUNIOR
          What happened to your computer?

                    PENNY
          It broke.

                    JUNIOR
          It was working fine the other day.

A click is heard offscreen, JUNIOR turns his head to face her.

                    PENNY
               (Fanning the picture, and looking at
               it)
          Aww look at you.

He reaches for the picture, but he's too slow.

                    JUNIOR
          Give it.

                    PENNY
          Nope.

He's still reaching for the picture.

                    JUNIOR
          Forreal Penny it's not funny.

                    PENNY
          It's just a picture.

                    JUNIOR
          I don't like getting my picture taken.

                    PENNY
               (Jaw dropped)
          What do you mean you don't like getting
          your picture taken?

JUNIOR looks into the water.

                    JUNIOR
          I just don't like the way I look in them.

                    PENNY
          You think you're ugly?

JUNIOR nods his head.

                    PENNY
          You are not ugly. Now Ryan in our theater
          class he is ugly, but you, there is nothing
          wrong with how you look.

JUNIOR laughs.

                    PENNY
          I'm serious, I mean his face is ugly and
          the way he acts just makes it 10 times
          worse.

                    JUNIOR
          Do you think your mom is ugly?

The smile vanishes from PENNY's face.

                    PENNY
               (Pause)

> She used to be. But she's been ugly for so
> long that I don't even remember how she
> looked.

She looks at the water and snaps a picture.

                    JUNIOR
          Let's take one together.

                    PENNY
          Forreal?

                    JUNIOR
          Not really. But for you I'll do it.

That smile comes back to PENNY's face, she leans in
closer to JUNIOR. She smiles while he keeps a
straight face.

CLICK. The picture pops out and she shakes it. She
looks at the picture.

                    PENNY
          Nope we're doing this again, what kind of
          smile is this. Please smile.

She leans back over and JUNIOR has a big smile.
PENNY looks over at him for a beat admiring it. She
looks back into the camera and takes the photo. She
shakes the picture again.

                    PENNY
          Now that's a picture. You can keep this
          one. I'll keep the old one.

He takes the picture and looks at it, loving what he
sees. A snowball is thrown at him.

PENNY stands there with another in hand ready to be
launched.

                    JUNIOR

          Penny don't even think-

Another snowball hits him. He gets up and starts
grabbing a snowball, chasing her around. The two of
them are just laughing and enjoying each other on
this cold day.

INT. FAMILY HOUSE - EVENING

JUNIOR comes through the door, the family is all
around the table laughing and talking. He walks
closer to the kitchen seeing that his UNCLE HENRY
(early 60S) is at the table. EARL and MICHELLE sit
at the table with him. His mother is at the stove
cooking. A big water jug filled with liquor sits in
front of UNCLE HENRY.

                    HENRY
          Heyyy boy, where you been at?

He stares at him for a bit.

                    EARL
          Come on over here and speak to your uncle.

He walks over to his uncle and everyone watches him.
He gets close holding his hand out, the uncle grabs
it and pulls him closer giving him a big hug.

                    HENRY
          Ahh man, you need to eat some more. When
          you get bigger you can come down and work
          for me.

                    EARL
          Your uncle got a lot of land down the
          country, he make big money.

                    MICHELLE
          How much money you make?

                    RUTH
          Michelle you know better than that.

                    HENRY
              (Laughing)
          It's ok Ruth.
              (Reaching in his pocket)
          In fact. I make more than enough.

He pulls out a huge wad of bills. Everyone around
the table is in awe.

                    EARL
          Just say the word and we're down there.

                    HENRY
          Just hang tight baby bruh.

He flicks off a few bills and gives some to both
JUNIOR and MICHELLE.

                    HENRY
          Y'all get yourselves some candy or
          something.

                    RUTH
          And how's Randy and the rest of the family
          doing?

                    UNCLE HENRY
          They doing good and he doing good too when
          he ain't on that bottle talkin crazy.

                    RUTH
          Talkin crazy how?

                    EARL
          I'm serious Henry, just let us know and
          we'll be down there.

He scoots his chair back gets up and starts walking
towards the door. EARL does the same.

                    HENRY
          I got to get going now.

                    RUTH
          The food is almost done.

                    EARL
          Yeah get you something to eat.

                    HENRY
          I gotta go back down there tonight, I got
          some business to take care of in the
          morning.

They get to the door.

                    EARL
          I'm serious Henry, I can help you out a lot
          down there just give me a chance.

                    HENRY
          I got you baby bruh.

He opens the door and closes it. EARL looks at the
door fighting the urge to open it back up and follow
his brother. He turns to look at his family, crammed
up in this small apartment, ashamed at the sight. He
walks past them and into the bedroom shutting the
door behind him.

INT. JOHN THOMAS MIDDLE SCHOOL - CLASSROOM - DAY

                    MR. ROWE
          For this next assignment you will be
          working in partners, and in your partners
          you will be given a scene, that you and
          your partner must perform to the class.

The teacher continues explaining the lesson, JUNIOR
is drawing in his notebook. He sits alone, PENNY is
absent.

The door opens and his head shoots up towards it.

Another student walks in; it's not PENNY.

His head goes back to his notebook.

                    MR. ROWE
          Ok, find your partners.

The kids in the classroom all find their partners,
handshakes and smiles between the pairs.

JUNIOR doesn't move.

MR. ROWE walks up to JUNIOR sitting beside him.

                    MR. ROWE
          When's the last time you seen Penny? It's
          not like her to miss this many days.

JUNIOR doesn't say anything, nor does he give eye
contact. MR. ROWE reaches for and closes JUNIOR'S
journal.

                    MR. ROWE
          If she doesn't show up, you're going to
          have to work with someone else.

                    JUNIOR
          She'll show.

MR. ROWE takes a deep breath, gets ups and walks
over to the next group.

JUNIOR looks at PENNY'S empty chair. Curious and
slightly worried.

INT. JOHN THOMAS MIDDLE SCHOOL - CAFETERIA - MOMENTS
LATER

JUNIOR is eating his lunch and he looks across the
cafeteria. MICHELLE is still with the same group of
people, a boy beside her rubbing on her leg but
MICHELLE doesn't do anything.

JUNIOR shakes his head and goes back to eating. CJ
and his followers sit in front of him.

                    CJ
          Where Penny been at?

JUNIOR ignores him.

                    CJ
          You think she gonna let me fuck?

                    FOLLOWER 1
          You don't want that her and mom be sharing
          drugs and shit.

They laugh.

                    CJ
          That's where she at? I knew she stinked and
          all but I ain't know she was doing drugs
          too.

JUNIOR is still silent. CJ reaches across and grabs
food from JUNIOR'S plate eating it. He looks at
MICHELLE, who is now secretly kissing the boy beside
her, oblivious to what's going on. CJ notices JUNIOR
looking behind him, he turns around and notices the
same thing.

                    CJ
          You know Gregory crushing that right? You
          think she gonna let me fuck next.

His followers laugh.

                    CJ
          Damn you a bitch and she's a hoe.

He takes one more item off of JUNIOR'S tray and walks away. The lunch bell rings. MICHELLE sees the bullies walking off, she gets up and walks over to JUNIOR who is gathering his stuff quickly walking away.

                    MICHELLE
          Hey are you ok?

He keeps walking ignoring her. She follows him out of the cafeteria.

INT. JOHN THOMAS MIDDLE SCHOOL - FRONT DOOR

He's headed towards the front door.

                    MICHELLE
          JUNIOR, where are you going?

He gets to the door, opens it and runs out.

                    MICHELLE
              (Shouting)
          JUNIOR!

MICHELLE watches as he runs away.

INT. TIGER MART - MOMENTS LATER

A bunch of junk food scattered all over the counter. The cashier rings it up. There is commotion going on out front. JUNIOR peaks out the door, his gaze stuck on something.

A woman, disheveled and desperate, arguing with a man.

                    CASHIER
          10.50.

A beat of watching, he studies this woman, knowing
her from somewhere.

                    CASHIER
          Kid. 10.50.

JUNIOR continues to look while he reaches in his
pocket. He pulls out a 20 dollar bill sliding it
along the counter. The cashier gives JUNIOR his
change and he walks off.

The woman outside looks through the glass back at
JUNIOR and then towards the money that's being
handed back to him.

EXT. TIGER MART - CONTINUOUS

We hear the argument clearly now. JUNIOR is walking
away but we can still hear it in the distance.

                    WOMAN
          Come on man. You know I'm good for it.

                    DEALER
          You ain't good for shit. It took you three
          weeks to pay me back, I ain't finna get
          killed cause I'm given out handouts.

                    WOMAN
          Please.

                    DEALER
               (Temper Rising)
          Either you come back with some money or
          step off.

JUNIOR has gotten a good distance from the pair.

                    WOMAN
          Hey baby.

He keeps walking.

                    WOMAN
          Baby wait up.

He stops, the woman continues to walk closer to him.

                    WOMAN
          Yes I'm talking to you.

He turns around completely. The woman is now
standing in front of him, with no regard to his
personal space. They lock eyes.

                    WOMAN
          Where I know you from?

Silence from JUNIOR, he looks at her with pure
disgust. She looks at him from head to toe, really
thinking, and it hits her.

                    WOMAN
          You that boy that be hanging with my Penny.

JUNIOR looks down.

                    PENNY'S MOM
          Yeah that's it. I know you, you don't think
          I pay attention but I do.
               (Beat)
          Can you do me a favor and help me out? I
          know you got some change on you.

                    JUNIOR
               (Turning away)
          I ain't got nothing for you.

He walks away from her, she is still behind him, her
desperation building.

                    PENNY'S MOM

> You think you're different than all these
> other dudes out here, well let me tell you
> you're not. You gonna grow up to be scared
> and weak just like them.

We stay on PENNY'S MOM, her breathing becoming
heavy, realizing her chance of getting that money is
fleeting.

                    PENNY'S MOM
               (Then)
          YOU STAY AWAY FROM PENNY. YOU HEAR ME. YOU
          WILL NEVER SEE HER AGAIN.

This stops him in his tracks.

                    PENNY'S MOM
          If you want to keep seeing her let me hold
          something. And don't say you don't got no
          money cause I saw the man give you change.

She walks closer to him.

                    PENNY'S MOM
          I'm just gonna buy food, just let me hold
          something, and you can spend as much time
          with her as you want.

He thinks on it, a smile comes across her face
revealing her stained chipped teeth.

He reaches into his pocket and pulls out the ten
dollar bill. She's trying to hold her excitement in,
her plan worked. She snatches the bill.

                    PENNY'S MOM
               (Laughing)
          When you see Penny tell her that I'm
          looking for her.

She runs back down the street to the dealer,
flagging him down.

We stay on JUNIOR while he walks away, in the background PENNY's MOM gives the dealer the money, a runner comes and gives her the drugs she walks into an alley.

EXT. PENNY'S HOUSE - LATER

JUNIOR stands in front of PENNY'S evicted house, all of their belongings abandoned outside. He walks up to the pile of stuff and sorts through it. He notices their picture on the ground. He grabs it and looks now knowing exactly where she is.

EXT. ANACOSTIA RIVER (THE SPOT) - CONTINUOUS

PENNY sits looking at the water. Her clothes are beat up, hair not done, it's been a rough week.

JUNIOR approaches her and slowly sits beside her. She doesn't move. He stares into her eyes, she can't hold it in any longer, the tears fall down her face nonstop.

He instantly pulls her close.

                    JUNIOR
          It's ok. It's ok.

Both of their backs facing us, PENNY's head resting on JUNIOR's shoulders sobbing. JUNIOR'S embrace and silence provides all the comfort she needs.

EXT. FAMILY HOUSE - FRONT DOOR - LATER

JUNIOR opens the front door to his house.

                    JUNIOR
               (To Penny)
          You can sit right here.

                    PENNY
          Are your parents ok with this?

                    JUNIOR
          I'm about to ask right now.

MICHELLE walks from the backroom.

                    MICHELLE
          Don't bother, they went down the country.

                    JUNIOR
          Ok, good. Penny is gonna stay here for a
          couple days. Are there extra towels and-

                    MICHELLE
          She can't stay here.

They all look at Michelle, the room is silent.

                    JUNIOR
          She's not leaving.

                    MICHELLE
          Yeah she is.

                    JUNIOR
          Where is she supposed to go Michelle?

                    MICHELLE
          SHE. IS. NOT. STAYING. HERE.

PENNY gets up and walks towards the door.

                    PENNY
          I don't need this.

                    JUNIOR
          Penny wait.

                    MICHELLE
          Yeah go ahead and leave.

                    PENNY
          Fuck you.

                    MICHELLE
          What did you just say to me?

PENNY opens the door and slams it behind her. JUNIOR
goes after her.

                    MICHELLE
          Where do you think you're going?

                    JUNIOR
          I'm getting Penny.

He opens up the door and MICHELLE comes from behind.
She shuts the door back and then stands in front of
it.

                    JUNIOR
          MOVE!

                    MICHELLE
          No, I am not going to let that girl hurt
          you.

                    JUNIOR
          She isn't hurting me.

                    MICHELLE
          I'm your sister, I know what's best for
          you.

                    JUNIOR
          She is more of a sister than you could ever
          be.

                    MICHELLE
               (BEAT)

You think she likes you? Nobody likes you
JUNIOR. Y'all are just hanging together
because nobody likes either of you. Can't
you see that. She's using you so she can
feel better.

                    JUNIOR
          (Opening the door)
You saying anything now.

                    MICHELLE
          (Closing the door)
Are you that pressed to fit in?

                    JUNIOR
Look who's talking.

                    MICHELLE
What?

                    JUNIOR
You don't think I see how those boys be
touching all on you, rubbing you and
kissing you. That's how you want to fit in
by being a hoe.

                    MICHELLE
I'm not a hoe.

                    JUNIOR
Just shut up and leave me alone.

He heads towards the door. MICHELLE snaps. She
lunges towards JUNIOR grabbing him and throwing him
to the ground.

                    MICHELLE
Now whose the hoe, you better watch who you
talking to cause I'm all you got.

JUNIOR jumps up and tackles MICHELLE. They tussle on the ground. JUNIOR digs deep, he picks her up and presses her out against a wall, holding her by the collar. He's stronger than she thinks, she can't move. The savagery begins to show in JUNIOR's eyes.

                    JUNIOR
          YOU THINK YOU KNOW.

                    MICHELLE
          JUNIOR, YOU'RE HURTING ME.

                    JUNIOR
          This is what you wanted right, you wanted
          me to be tough, you wanted me to be a man
          right.

                    MICHELLE
          JUNIOR.

                    JUNIOR
          I told you to stop fucking with me.

JUNIOR draws his fist back, MICHELLE closes her eyes preparing for the hit. He doesn't swing.

He moves his hand from her collar and walks towards the door leaving the house. MICHELLE slides down the wall putting her head between her legs breathing heavily and crying.

EXT. SAVANNAH ST. WASHINGTON, D.C. - EVENING

JUNIOR is running down the street calling out for PENNY. He gets no responses. He makes it to the corner of the street and sees PENNY standing at the bus stop. He sprints to her as the bus comes to a stop and the doors open. PENNY tries to get on the bus but JUNIOR grabs her by the arm.

                    JUNIOR

Penny wait.

                    PENNY
Don't touch me.

                    JUNIOR
Come back to the house.

                    PENNY
Your sister doesn't want me there. My mom
doesn't want me, nobody wants me.

                    JUNIOR
I want you. I got you I told you that.

                    BUS DRIVER.
Come on man, we don't got all day.

She thinks about it.

                    JUNIOR
Trust me.

She walks off the bus and it pulls off leaving the
two of them alone at the stop.

INT. FAMILY HOUSE - NIGHT

A montage of events leading up to them going to
sleep.

PENNY getting in the shower, the water pouring on
her hair and body. The dirt from her body mixes with
the water, going down into the drain.

JUNIOR putting a pot on a burner, pouring a can of
soup into it.

He walks into his bedroom and grabs a t-shirt and
shorts for PENNY to sleep in. MICHELLE sits on the
bed watching him, she lays down as he exits.

They both sit down at the table. PENNY is eating and JUNIOR is sitting with her, telling her a story. He is animated, and goofy. PENNY is engaged and laughing.

They watch TV devouring the snacks that JUNIOR had bought earlier.

PENNY lays down on the couch, pulling the blanket over her.

JUNIOR sits on the ground beside her.

                    JUNIOR
          Are you ok?

                    PENNY
          Yes.

She sits up.

                    PENNY
          Why are you so nice to me?

                    JUNIOR
          We all deserve someone to be nice to us.

                    PENNY
          I don't know where I'd be without you.

She reaches over and gives him a big hug. He hugs her back.

                                        CUT TO:

INT. KIDS BEDROOM - CONTINUOUS

MICHELLE peeking through her bedroom door looking at them hug, she slowly shuts the door.

Off Screen we hear

                    JUNIOR (O.S.)

Do you love me?

FADE TO:

INT. JOHN THOMAS MIDDLE SCHOOL - CLASSROOM - DAY

JUNIOR and PENNY are acting out their play in front
of the classroom. They are passionate and deep into
their characters. PENNY is a natural actor, while
JUNIOR'S confidence grows with each line. They are
sitting down, PENNY resting her head on JUNIOR'S
shoulders.

                    PENNY
          Of course, why would you ask me that?

                    JUNIOR
          No, like do you love me the way that I love
          you.

                    PENNY
          How do you love me?

                    JUNIOR
          I can't describe it.

                    PENNY
          Can you try?

JUNIOR sits up and turns his shoulders towards PENNY
staring into her eyes.

                    JUNIOR
          At this moment I wish that we could be
          together, not as friends but as something
          more.

                    PENNY
          How long have you been thinking about this?

                    JUNIOR
          For a minute.

                    PENNY
               (Pause)
     You do know that I'm getting married
     tomorrow right?

                    THE CLASS (O.S.)
     Ouuuuu.

They both smile a bit shocked at how good they are
doing.

                    PENNY
     Why would you wait until the day before my
     wedding to tell me this?

                    JUNIOR
     Well what did you want me to do?

                    PENNY
     You could've just told me.

                    JUNIOR
     And what if you didn't feel the same way.

                    PENNY
     But I did.

Pause.

                    JUNIOR
     Did?

                    PENNY
     Did. As in I use to, but not anymore.

                    JUNIOR
     That's not true. I know that deep down you
     still love me.

                    PENNY
     Why are you doing this? What do you want me
     to do?

                    JUNIOR
          Marry me.

The class gasps.

                    PENNY
          What?

                    JUNIOR
          Right here. Right now.

She turns to walk away.

                    JUNIOR
          Wait.

                    PENNY
          No that's not how this works, you can't
          just do that.

                    JUNIOR
          Can I at least read you my vows?

                    PENNY
          You wrote vows?

JUNIOR goes in his pocket and pulls out a sheet of
paper.

                    JUNIOR
          As I stand in front you I realized that
          there isn't enough words to describe how
          much I love you. I want to spend everyday
          with you and I promise that I will give you
          my all, and make sure that you are happy
          every single day. I will be by your side
          forever and always. I love you.

The classroom is dead silent, anticipating what's
next

PENNY walks away, JUNIOR follows her turning her around and giving her a big hug, they look at each other as if they are going to kiss and after a few beats.

                    PENNY & JUNIOR
          AND SCENE.

The class gives them a round of applause. MR. ROWE wipes his face.

                    MR. ROWE
          Now that's what I'm talking about, amazing
          work you two.

They take a bow and walk back to their seats.

                    MR. ROWE
          Now we have Tyler and Jacob.

                    TYLER
          I'm not going after that.

                    MR. ROWE
          Just try your best.

The Guidance Counselor knocks on the door.

                    GUIDANCE COUNSELOR
          Hey Mr. Rowe I need to see Penny for a
          second.

                    MR. ROWE
          Yeah of course.

PENNY scoots her chair out and walks out to talk to the Guidance Counselor.

The door is shut but you can still see them through the glass. Tyler and Jacob have begun their scene, it's an improv cops and robbers scene.

Our attention is still on the door, the Counselor
has her hand on PENNY's shoulders talking to her.

JUNIOR looks at the window trying to read her lips.
By their mannerisms something is clearly wrong. They
walk away from in front of the closed door. We stay
on JUNIOR's face. The boys' performance begins to
fade out...

...another sound rising-- the river, crickets,
busses and cars driving from afar.

                                        CUT TO:

EXT. ANACOSTIA RIVER (THE SPOT) - LATER

PENNY and JUNIOR sit at their spot with a deep
silence between them, they've been like this for
hours.

                    PENNY
          They found her in the back of an alley. She
          had been dead for a week.

JUNIOR looks at her, trying to come up with
something to say.

                    JUNIOR
          Penny I-

                    PENNY
          The last time she was seen she was at the
          Tiger Mart begging a kid for money. This
          kid had on a red jacket, with a bag full of
          stuff.

JUNIOR realizing where she's getting at, shifting
his gaze.

                    PENNY

Did you see my mom that day, before you
came here?

JUNIOR'S face. Crushed. He nods.

                    PENNY
          You gave her money?

JUNIOR'S head falls, his answer revealed in his
silence.

She rises and without saying a word she walks away.
JUNIOR stays seated, unable to move, to speak.

                                        CUT TO:

INT. JOHN THOMAS MIDDLE SCHOOL - CAFETERIA - DAY

JUNIOR sits by himself at the lunch table he is
doodling in his journal.

We see JUNIOR'S drawing. It's a picture of him and
PENNY in their spot with "I'M SORRY" written in big
bold letters.

INT. JOHN THOMAS MIDDLE SCHOOL - SCHOOL YARD - DAY

JUNIOR is leaving out of the school building in a
rush, he walks down the stairs. CJ trips him up and
he goes tumbling down the steps. His papers fall
everywhere and his journal lands on the ground.

CJ walks towards the journal and looks inside,
ripping out the picture.

MICHELLE comes and helps him up.

                    JUNIOR
          Give it back.

                    CJ
          (Showing it to his followers)

Aww look.

                    MICHELLE
          (Standing in CJ's face)
     GIVE IT BACK.

                    CJ
          (Looking at JUNIOR)
     Ok.

CJ rips the picture in half.

                    CJ
     Now he has two of them.

JUNIOR lunges at CJ tackling him to the ground.
Another bully tries to rush JUNIOR but MICHELLE
steps in pushing him back and then punching him in
the face. The boy throws another blow which MICHELLE
ducks and hits him again.

JUNIOR is on top of CJ throwing wild power punches
that all land on CJ's face.

More of his followers come hitting JUNIOR on his
head and body. He is taking all of these punches
trying his best to fight through the pain.

Police sirens sound off in the distance and the kids
disperse.

MICHELLE yanks JUNIOR by the collar but he doesn't
move. JUNIOR turns his head to face her, these
aren't the soft eyes from earlier. His eyes now
filled with rage and pain.

MICHELLE yanks him again harder and they start to
run home not looking back or stopping.

INT. FAMILY HOUSE - FRONT DOOR - CONTINUOUS

The door flies open and they enter. They are both
out of breath, bloody and dirty.

JUNIOR goes to sit on the couch. Michelle walks over
to him and examines his face. He winces at the pain.

                    MICHELLE
          Ima get you some ice. You'll be alright.

MICHELLE walks away from JUNIOR.

                    MICHELLE
               (Hype)
          That's what I'm talkin bout. I knew you
          wasn't weak. It feels good knowing that you
          just whooped someones ass.

INT. BATHROOM - CONTINUOUS

She walks to the bathroom to check her face.

                    MICHELLE
          Just cause ima girl don't mean that I can't
          fight niggas. I don't do that grabbing hair
          shit I throw straight hands.

She walks out of the bathroom, and into the kitchen.

INT. FAMILY HOUSE (KITCHEN) - CONTINUOUS

She opens the fridge and grabs some frozen peas and
some juice. She gets two cups and pours juice into
them.

                    MICHELLE
          I'm proud of you. You should've seen
          yourself, you was teeing off on CJ. What
          you think?

She stops, waiting for a response but she doesn't
get one.

                    MICHELLE
          Junior?

A beat of confusion. MICHELLE grabs the cups and
walks out of the kitchen and into the living room.

                    MICHELLE
          Junior, do you hear me?

JUNIOR is laying down on the couch. She walks up to
him.

                    MICHELLE
               (Laughing)
          Come on Junior wake up I just poured you
          some juice.

She taps him but he doesn't move.

                    MICHELLE
          Junior?

She shakes him harder and he slumps over. She drops
the juice and grabs him with two hands. Her anxiety
turned into full panic.

                    MICHELLE
          NO NO NO NO NO JUNIOR. COME ON JUNIOR WAKE
          UP. PLEASE COME ON JUNIOR STOP PLAYING
          PLEASE COME ON WAKE UP.

She rushes over to the phone and calls the police.
She gives them their address and leaves the phone
dangling. She goes back to JUNIOR trying to get him
to wake up. He doesn't.

She holds him tight crying and pleading, as we...

                                        CUT TO BLACK.

Over black we hear... the sounds of an EKG machine, slowly beeping and small chatter that's not distinctive.

                                        FADE IN:

INT. HOSPITAL ROOM - A FEW DAYS LATER

JUNIOR'S eyes slowly opened up, a bandage on his cheek and a couple stitches on his forehead. His face is bruised badly and his eye is swollen. He turns his head to examine the room. His mom is outside the door talking to a nurse.

He looks to his right and MICHELLE is asleep in a chair.

                    JUNIOR
               (Weak)
          Michelle. Michelle.

She picks her head up slowly, waking up. She smiles and walks over to her brother sitting beside him. She gives him a hug and he grunts in pain.

                    MICHELLE
          I'm sorry. You scared the hell out of me. I
          knew you were going to be ok. You were
          sleep for two-

                    JUNIOR
          Where's Penny?

MICHELLE pauses.

                    JUNIOR
          I have to tell her I'm sorry.

                    MICHELLE
               (Pause)
          Penny doesn't go to our school anymore.

JUNIOR looks at her in shock.

> MICHELLE
> I heard she moved to North Carolina with her aunt.

He can't look at her anymore, his lips begin to quiver, tears forming in his eyes.

> MICHELLE
> Junior. Moms been asking, and I've been trying to come up with something to tell her but I just can't, why were those boys always messing with you?

JUNIOR looks straight ahead, the tears now uncontrollably falling from his face.

> JUNIOR
> (Crying)
> I don't know. I don't know why people keep messing with me.

Pause, he is breaking down, sobbing. He pulls himself together slightly.

> JUNIOR
> What am I doing that's so wrong? Is it because I'm ugly? Is it because of my clothes? What is it? Why do people keep messing with me?

He's tried to fight it long enough but the tears come back.

> JUNIOR
> I can't take it anymore Michelle. I just can't take it.

MICHELLE grabs him and pulls him close to her. In her arms her brother cries tears of pain, and of sorrow.

We stay with these siblings. JUNIOR finally being able to get it all out and MICHELLE giving him the space to do that. Amongst the cries we hear those three words.

                    MICHELLE
          I'm here now.

These cries can still be heard while we...

                              FADE TO BLACK.

          END OF ACT III: WINTER

The sounds of chatter begin to rise, through it all we hear a familiar voice. However it's distorted and dreamlike as if it's playing in someone's mind.

                    JUNIOR
               (Crying, pleading)
          Michelle. Michelle. Michelle please.
          Michelle.

MICHELLE jumps out of her sleep drenched in sweat. She turns to her bed side to see JUNIOR isn't right beside her.

INT. FAMILY HOUSE (LIVING ROOM) - MORNING

JUNIOR sits on the couch watching TV, no expression, just a blank stare.

MICHELLE walks past him dressed in her uniform and heading towards the door. She looks at her brother one last time. She opens the door and leaves.

INT. JOHN THOMAS MIDDLE SCHOOL - CAFETERIA - DAY

MICHELLE is sitting at the table with her normal group of friends, no boy beside her this time. She is spaced out, looking at CJ across the cafeteria, he nods his head to her, a hate filled respect lingers between them. MICHELLE rolls her eyes disgusted.

                    RANAE
          MICHELLE.

She looks at RANAE.

                    RANAE
          You ok?

                    MICHELLE
          Yeah I'm good.

The kids continue their conversation but MICHELLE pays them no mind.

EXT. JOHN THOMAS MIDDLE SCHOOL - SCHOOL YARD - LATER

The school day has ended, MICHELLE is walking out of the door. MR. ROWE with papers in his hands calls her from behind and she stops.

                    MR. ROWE
          Hey. Are you ok?

                    MICHELLE
          Yes.

                    MR. ROWE
                (A slight pause)
          How is JUNIOR doing?

She goes silent.

                    MR. ROWE
          That bad huh?
                (Slight Pause)

            Well look
                    (handing MICHELLE paper)
          We're having this 10 minute play festival
          at the school next month. I would love for
          JUNIOR to be apart of it, he's really
          talented.

                              MICHELLE
                        (Grabbing the paper)
          I didn't know JUNIOR could act.

                              MR. ROWE
          He can do alot of things Michelle. Tell him
          I said hello.

MR. ROWE walks away, MICHELLE folds the paper and
puts it in her jacket pocket.

INT. FAMILY HOUSE - CONTINUOUS

MICHELLE walks through the door, their mother is on
the phone moving quickly with items in her hand.
Overwhelmed.

                              MICHELLE
          What's going on?

                              RUTH
          We're going down the country tomorrow.

                              MICHELLE
          Why?

                              RUTH
          Your uncle Randy died.

                              MICHELLE
          What? How?

                              RUTH

We are still figuring everything out. Go
pack your bag.

MICHELLE turns to head to her room.

                    RUTH (O.S.)
          And help your brother too.

INT. KIDS BEDROOM - CONTINUOUS

MICHELLE stands in the threshold looking at JUNIOR
laying down in the bed. He's not sleep, his eyes are
open and he feels MICHELLE'S presence.

                    JUNIOR
          I can do it myself. I don't need your help.

                    MICHELLE
          You heard mom, she told me to help you.

She takes off her jacket and backpack, dropping it
to the floor and she walks over to JUNIOR'S drawer.

                    JUNIOR
               (Sitting up)
          I said I can do it myself. I'm not weak I
          can handle things.

                    MICHELLE
          I know you can JUNIOR.

                    JUNIOR
          You're just being sarcastic.

She walks away upset, shutting the door behind her.
He gets up and heads towards the drawer. As he
begins to take clothes out, he looks down noticing a
piece of paper from MICHELLE'S jacket pocket. It's
the flier that MR. ROWE gave her. After reading it
he balls it up and tosses it towards a trash can.

INT./EXT. CAR - THE NEXT DAY

The family is piled into a decent size car heading
to DANVILLE, VA or THE COUNTRY. EARL is at the
wheel, their mother is in the passenger seat, and
the kids are in the back.

The apartment complexes and large gatherings of
people have given way to rural plains and large
acres of land filled with animals. The skies are
wide, no helicopters, planes, or sirens are heard.

They are no longer on a regular road as the car
rumbles against the dirt and rock covered roads of
THE COUNTRY.

The tires ease to a stop as they reach...

EXT. EARL CHILDHOOD HOME - DAY

A small shack of a house. It is better than their
old destroyed house that rests in the backyard.

There is a dirt path that leads to three different
tobacco fields and another house that is owned by
another member of the family.

EARL'S sisters ANNE (early 60s) and MARIE (MID 50s)
are sitting on chairs in front of the house. There
is also a pack of dogs roaming around the grounds.

The car door flings open and the family gets out.
The aunts make their way to them.

                    ANNE
          Oh my goodness, look how big yall gotten.
          Come over here and give me a hug.

ANNE gives them both a warm southern hug and MARIE
does the same.

                    MARIE

> We missed y'all so much.

They then give their mother a hug.

                    ANNE
          How you doing Ruth?

                    RUTH
          I'm ok, how are you?

                    ANNE
          We're ok around here, we just trying to
          figure everything out.

                    EARL
          Where Henry?

                    MARIE
          Don't you start that up again, you drove me
          crazy during the winter with all this land
          stuff.

                    EARL
              (Irritated)
          Shit.

He leaves the group and goes into the house.

                    RUTH
              (To Anne)
          Don't mind him.

                    ANNE
          I ain't worried bout him at all. Y'all come
          get out this heat. We got some food
          cooking, it's gonna be done in a few hours.

They all walk into the house.

INT. KITCHEN/DINING ROOM - EVENING

The adults are at the main table. Pig feet, chicken, greens and a bunch of other southern foods are being passed around.

The kids are tucked away at a smaller table far from the conversation.

ANNE walks over to the kids table. MICHELLE and JUNIOR still have plates that have barely been touched, only eating what they recognize.

                    ANNE
          Y'all need to eat before it gets cold, we
          don't waste food over here.

ANNE walks back to the adult table and takes her seat. At the head of the table is BIG MOMMA (late 90s) she is lighter than the rest of her children. She's slouched over, not saying much while MARIE feeds her. FLORENE, RUTH and EARL'S younger brother ISSAC are all at the table.

                    MARIE
          We gonna get Randy body tomorrow, we gonna
          put him in one of his good suits. Earl,
          Issac, y'all make the casket, and Henry
          gonna dig the grave

                    RUTH
          Which suit?

                    ISSAC
          It gotta be the blue one, he liked the
          blue.

                    FLORENE
          And make sure you make the cross real
          special like.

                    EARL
          What happened to him?

                    MARIE
          Not at the table.

                    EARL
          Seem like everyone else know.

                    ANNE
          He got shot Earl.

A silence falls at the table, everyone processing in
their own way. Big Momma doesn't react, she keeps
chewing her food, accustomed to death.

                    EARL
          Who did it?

                    ANNE
          They found him up the road, ain't nobody
          been saying nothing bout it.

                    EARL
          Who was the last person that saw him?

                    FLORENE
          Henry was the last person to see him.

Silence.

                    EARL
          I'm sure Henry is gonna need an extra hand
          on the farm now.

                    ANNE
          Earl what is wrong with you?

EARL looks around the table to see that everyone is
upset with him. He gets up from the table in
frustration, walking out of the door.

                    RUTH
          I'm sorry.

                    MARIE

Nothing to be sorry about. That land is
just getting to them.

                    FLORENE
That land is the worst thing that could've
happened to this family. It's driving them
apart.

INT. BEDROOM - NIGHT

With a window open, the sounds of a night in The
COUNTRY dominate the room. Crickets chirping, snakes
hissing and the occasional howl of a dog.

The kids are on their knees reciting a prayer.

                    JUNIOR & MICHELLE
Now I lay me down to sleep. I pray the Lord
my soul to keep if I should die before I
wake, I pray the Lord my soul to take.
AMEN.

Their mother watches from the door smiling.

                    FLORENE
Goodnight y'all.

                    JUNIOR & MICHELLE
                 (Not together exactly)
Goodnight.

Off FLORENE, their mother comes and tucks them in,
giving them both a kiss on the cheek.

                    RUTH
Goodnight y'all.

She shuts out the light.

INT. BEDROOM - NIGHT

MICHELLE wakes up from her sleep, and goes out of the door.

INT. BATHROOM - CONTINUOUS

MICHELLE finishes using the bathroom. She goes to wash her hands but begins to hear familiar voices from an open window in the bathroom.

She walks to the window and stands up on her tip toes to look outside.

EXT. FRONT PORCH - CONTINUOUS

HENRY, ISSAC, and EARL are outside sitting on the porch. HENRY is pouring into his cup and the cup of his brothers.

He tosses the empty jug on the grass next to another two empty jugs.

> ISSAC
> This some good stuff here boy.

> HENRY
> Them people up the street aint gettin no more of my money.

> ISSAC
> They done lost they damn minds charging 20 dollars for a pint.

> HENRY
> Exactly that's why I started making my own.

INT. BATHROOM - CONTINUOUS

MICHELLE attentively listening.

EXT. FRONT PORCH - CONTINUOUS

                    EARL
What happened to Randy?

                    ISSAC
Now why you gonna do that? Aint you been
listenin he was shot.

                    HENRY
Yeah, he was shot.

                    EARL
Who shot him?

A beat of thought. HENRY finishes his drink.

                    HENRY
          (Finally)
He did.

                    EARL
What are you talking about?

                    HENRY
It mean what it mean, the nigga shot
himself.

The brothers are silent. HENRY reaches down beside
him and opens up another liquor filled jug, pouring
some into his cup.

                    EARL
You was suppose to be watchin him.

                    HENRY
          (After taking a sip)
He a grown man, I gotta business to run, I
can't make money and play caretaker for a
grown man.

                    ISSAC
That wasn't no regular man, that was our
brother. Your brother.

                    HENRY
          Blood or not, HE HIS OWN MAN.

                    ISSAC
          You was the last to see him though.

                    HENRY
          I saw him the day before, on the field
          talking crazy.

                    EARL
          What was he saying?

                    HENRY
          I don't remember.

                    ISSAC
          Come on Henry.

                    HENRY
          I said I don't remember what the fuck you
          want me to do. I helped him out, I gave him
          money, a job, I did all that I could.

                    ISSAC
          It ain't about the money Henry.

HENRY looks at his brothers resentfully and they
look back at him, unsure and without closure. He
downs his drink and reaches for his gallon jug.
Walking off the porch and onto the dirt trail, he
continues drinking as he vanishes into the night.

INT. BEDROOM - CONTINUOUS

MICHELLE is up looking at the ceiling fan trying to
make sense of everything that she's heard outside.
She looks at her brother again and almost
instinctively, she reaches for her brother's hands,
holding it tight.

EXT. OUTDOORS AROUND THE HOUSE - THE NEXT DAY

A rusty shovel is being dragged across the dirt
trail and then onto a grassy field.A liquid jug
swishing around.

It's HENRY.

He stops when he reaches a gravesite. A tombstone
that reads LAVAN SMITH and beside it, another grave
that reads JESSE SMITH.

He uses his feet to measure out how far he should
dig the grave. He reaches a spot and attempts to
break ground. The ground is resistant at first but
he uses all of this strength, finally breaking
through.

EARL and ISSAC carry wood to a small shack in the
back of the house. It is filled with tools. They
start cutting the wood, carefully putting together
the casket.

INT. FAMILY HOUSE (KITCHEN) - CONTINUOUS

ANNE, MARIE and FLORENE pick out RANDY's clothes
placing them neatly on the bed.

FLORENE and RUTH are cooking and BIG MOMMA sits on a
chair in the living room.

MICHELLE and JUNIOR stand in front of a clock and
watch the time pass by. It is 11:59 A.M. The
secondhand maneuvers around the clock, it strikes 12
and a bird springs out, CUCKOOING extremely loud.
The kids look unamused, they've been doing this for
hours.

                    JUNIOR
                (Walking away)
          I'm going to the bathroom.

>   MICHELLE
>   The toilet is clogged you have to use to
>   the outhouse.

>   JUNIOR
>   I literally just used it a few hours ago.

>   MICHELLE
>   I guess those chitlins ran through Aunt
>   Florene.

He grabs toilet paper and heads outside. MICHELLE
follows behind.

>   MICHELLE
>   Watch out for the snakes.

>   JUNIOR
>   Leave me alone Michelle.

>   MICHELLE
>   If a snake bites you I'm not sucking the
>   venom out of you.

JUNIOR walks toward the outhouse. MICHELLE hops down
from the top step and begins walking to the back of
the house.

>   JUNIOR
>   Where are you going?

>   MICHELLE
>   Exploring.

JUNIOR shifts his attention back to the tall grass
that sits between him and the outhouse. He walks
through slowly and carefully.

He opens the door to the outhouse and walks in to
use the bathroom.

EXT. BACK OF THE HOUSE - CONTINUOUS

MICHELLE walks to the back of the house. Behind it is the family's old house, the one that her grandfather and uncles built together. It's destroyed for the most part but it is still upright.

She walks up to the door and peeks through a hole. Looking down she sees a picture of all the brothers together smiling. She turns around to face the house seeing something in the distance that makes her smile.

EXT. FRONT PORCH

JUNIOR is walking back to the front porch from the outhouse. He stops when he sees MICHELLE holding up a bike.

                    JUNIOR
          Where'd you get that?

                    MICHELLE
          I found it around back. It's pretty old but
          it still works. We could take turns.

                    JUNIOR
              (Walking past her)
          I'm good.

                    MICHELLE
          Come on JUNIOR I'm tired of looking at the
          clock, I'm bored.

                    JUNIOR
          I don't know how to ride a bike.

                    MICHELLE
          Really?

                    JUNIOR
          Nobody would let me ride theirs and Penny's
          mom got rid of hers.

                    MICHELLE
          Well why did she-
               (Realizing)
          Oh.

He opens the door to the house.

                    MICHELLE
          I can teach you.

JUNIOR turns around.

                    MICHELLE
          Better than staring at the clock all day.

He looks at her still uncertain, but it is this same
uncertainty that brings a smile to his face.

                                        CUT TO:

EXT. DIRT ROAD - CONTINUOUS

MICHELLE is holding JUNIOR on the bike, he struggles
to keep his balance and pedal.

                    MICHELLE
          You got it, just stay straight.

                    JUNIOR
          I can't do this.

                    MICHELLE
          Yes you can.

JUNIOR continues to pedal and he begins to find his
groove balancing himself and staying upright.

                    MICHELLE
               (Excited)
          You got it. YOU GOT IT.

MICHELLE stops holding him and JUNIOR rides with no
support.

He is smiling, riding against the wind and enjoying
every second, lost within this brief moment of
ecstasy.

MICHELLE shouts behind him.

                    MICHELLE
          JUNIOR. JUNIOR HIT THE BRAKE.

He looks back at MICHELLE who is starting to run
behind him. He looks ahead and sees a huge log in
front of him. He quickly turns and loses control of
the bike, falling off rolling against the grass.

                    MICHELLE
                (Examining JUNIOR)
          Are you ok?

JUNIOR rolls over and is laughing hysterically.

                    MICHELLE
          Oh my god, I thought you were hurt.

                    JUNIOR
          Did you see me?

                    MICHELLE
          You learn quick. Your elbow.

JUNIOR looks at his elbow, it's a bit scraped up.

                    JUNIOR
                (Unfazed)
          I've had worse.

She smiles at him.

                    JUNIOR
                (Getting up)
          Come on lets go again.

                    MICHELLE
          You still ain't learn your lesson?

                    JUNIOR
          What lesson? That was fun.

JUNIOR grabs the bike and gets on it struggling.

                    JUNIOR
          I think I saw a badminton set back at the
          house.

                    MICHELLE
          Are you sure you're ready for that?

                    JUNIOR
          You aint better than me.

                    MICHELLE
          Ok we'll see.

                    JUNIOR
          Race you back to the house.

JUNIOR starts to peddle faster.

                    MICHELLE
               (Laughing)
          You're cheating.

JUNIOR'S foot slips off the pedal and he starts to
lose control again.

                    MICHELLE
               (Laughing)
          See that's what you get.

As the kids pedal off, UNCLE HENRY walks back toward
the grave to continue digging. He looks at the kids,
laughing and playing in the distance. He takes a big
gulp of his drink and looks down at the grave.

INT/EXT. DANVILLE - CONTINUOUS

A montage of events.

JUNIOR and MICHELLE play badminton in front of the house and they are both good at the game. It's competitive with lots of good natured trash-talk. MICHELLE swings and misses, JUNIOR throws the racket down in celebration.

They take turns riding the bike on the dirt road and all through the yard and fields.

The kids try on old clothes from the closet, most of them too big. MICHELLE walks down the hall mimicking a model down the runway, JUNIOR cheers her on.

MICHELLE and JUNIOR throw rocks into the tobacco field seeing who can throw it the furthest.

EXT. TOBACCO FIELD - CONTINUOUS

The sun is beginning to set, creating a beautiful hue of reds and oranges against the green tobacco fields.

JUNIOR and MICHELLE are lying down looking up at the clouds.

                    MICHELLE
               (Pointing up)
          What about that one?

                    JUNIOR
          Definitely a dinosaur.

                    MICHELLE
          What's up with you and dinosaurs?

                    JUNIOR
          I was joking the other times but don't you
          see the tail right there?

                    MICHELLE
          Actually, it looks like you.

                    JUNIOR
          You tryna joan?

                    MICHELLE
          No I'm serious, look thats your arms, and
          right there, well all of that right there
          is your big ass head.

They start laughing. MICHELLE shifts her gaze to
JUNIOR who is now lost in those clouds.

                    MICHELLE
          Junior? What do you want to be when you
          grow up?

JUNIOR doesn't respond and finally, after a few
beats.

                    JUNIOR
          Alive.

MICHELLE sits up and looks at him.

                    JUNIOR
          I just want to be alive, at this point
          that's all I want.

                    MICHELLE
          Why wouldn't you be?

                    JUNIOR
          I don't know.

MICHELLE looks at him. She's heartbroken by both the
answers and how serious he is. She tries to lock
eyes with him, but he just looks straight into the
fields.

                    MICHELLE

I don't know what I would do without you.

                    JUNIOR
You would be fine without me. You don't
even like me.

                    MICHELLE
Junior. I love you.

                    JUNIOR
Then why are you so mean to me?

MICHELLE tries to scoot over to cover the distance,
he notices this and slides further away.

                    JUNIOR
Everyone is always so mean. What have I
done that was so bad to make people want to
hurt me all the time.
        (Takes a deep breath)
I can take all of that, I really can. But
if you don't like me then what's the point.

                    MICHELLE
I'm sorry Junior. I am so sorry. I need you
here. I don't know what I'd do without you.

She scoots over one more time and hugs him. He
hesitates at first but finally gives in. He wraps
his arms around her and they embrace as the sun
continues its descent.

EXT. GRAVE SITE - THE NEXT DAY

The family is dressed in all black. EARL AND ISSAC
carry the casket with the help of HENRY who is drunk
and stumbling. They lower the casket into the dirt.

None of them are crying.

MICHELLE and JUNIOR are standing side by side. She looks down watching HENRY who has just taken a sip from his flask.

He walks over to the casket, looking down at his brother, he collapses, falling to his hands and knees crying.

His cries grow louder, the pain and guilt all coming out at once. Suddenly he vomits into the grave, and is now shouting. His words are unclear. EARL and ISSAC grab him and carry him back into the house.

His cries are heard from within the house. MICHELLE looks at JUNIOR who is afraid, grabs his hand and holds it tight.

Our last view is of BIG MOMMA, a tear slowly falling down her cheek. A once beautiful face now filled with the pain and heartache from life and what it has done to her family. She finds the strength, her blank expression changes as a single tear falls down her face.

                                        FADE TO:

EXT. SAVANNAH ST - AFTERNOON

MICHELLE and JUNIOR are walking down the street from school.

                    JUNIOR
          I'm thinking about entering in that play
          festival at school.

                    MICHELLE
          Really?

                    JUNIOR

Mr. Rowe said that he'll help me write
something. I just need a scene partner.

                    MICHELLE
Do you have anyone in mind?

                    JUNIOR
No. Penny was always my scene partner.

MICHELLE energy shifts, it's all in her expression.

                    JUNIOR
What's your problem with Penny?

                    MICHELLE
I don't have one.

                    JUNIOR
You don't have to lie to me.

                    MICHELLE
It's just.
        (Slight pause, building courage to
        say, then)
I felt that she was taking you away from
me. And you said that she was a better
sister than me.

                    JUNIOR
I shouldn't have said that.

                    MICHELLE
It's kind of true.

                    JUNIOR
No it's not. She was just there for me when
no one else wanted to be.

MICHELLE starts to look down, too disappointed and
ashamed in herself to give eye contact.

                    JUNIOR

But you're here now.

MICHELLE lifts her head up and gives him a hug.

                    MICHELLE
So what play are we doing?

                    JUNIOR
        (Shocked)
What?

                    MICHELLE
If this is something that you want to do
then I'll help you.

JUNIOR and MICHELLE look at each other and smile.

                    MICHELLE
You gotta beat me first.

MICHELLE takes off running down the street and
JUNIOR runs after her, the pair laughing.

INT. JOHN THOMAS MIDDLE SCHOOL - CLASSROOM

It's the end of the school day MICHELLE and JUNIOR
walk into MR. ROWE'S class. He is talking to a group
of students who have also stayed after.

                    JUNIOR
        Mr. Rowe.

He stops talking.

                    MR. ROWE
Hey Junior.

                    JUNIOR
I want to enter into the festival.

                    MR. ROWE
Do you have a partner?

MICHELLE comes from behind JUNIOR to standing
directly beside him.

                    JUNIOR
          Yeah I do.

A smile coming to MR. ROWE'S face.

                    MR. ROWE
          I have the perfect idea for you both.

                                        CUT TO:

INT. JOHN THOMAS MIDDLE SCHOOL - CLASSROOM- DAY

MICHELLE and JUNIOR are typing up their play with
MR. ROWE guiding them.

They are now rehearsing it in the classroom.

INT. FAMILY HOUSE

They are in the living room rehearsing, scripts in
hand and junk food everywhere. They put the scripts
down and are practicing slow dancing, laughing and
smiling while they do it.

INT. JOHN THOMAS MIDDLE SCHOOL - CAFETERIA

MICHELLE is helping decorate the stage for the
festival. She is hanging up fake trees, while JUNIOR
is moving the cafeteria tables out of the way and
setting up the chairs.

EXT. CARRYOUT - NIGHT

MICHELLE and JUNIOR are sitting in a carryout. Their backs are up against the glass. MICHELLE is drinking a half and half, while JUNIOR is up telling her a story. He is dramatic in his movements and facial expressions, MICHELLE can't help but to laugh.

Everything falls silent, all we hear is...

                    MICHELLE (V.O.)
               (In an old woman's voice light and
               sweet)
          What took you so long?

                    JUNIOR
               (In an old man's voice, raspy,
               fragile)
          I'm sorry, I don't move as fast as I used
          to.

A laughter from the crowd.

                                        CUT TO:

INT. JOHN THOMAS MIDDLE SCHOOL - CAFETERIA

It's show-night, the cafeteria looks nothing like we've seen it before. Parents, some faculty and students are in attendance. It's not a full house but they've gotten a great turnout.

MICHELLE and JUNIOR are up on stage. They are both dressed in the clothes that they found down in the country, the ones belonging to their aunts and uncles.

Two rocking chairs on stage, along with a small table that has two glasses of lemonade and an old vinyl player. MICHELLE has a stress ball in her hand squeezing it.

The stage lighting suggests that it's a sunset.

We've caught them towards the end of their play.

                    MICHELLE
          Which lemonade is that?

                    JUNIOR
          Yours is sugar free.

                    MICHELLE
          Sugar free? I hate this stuff.

                    JUNIOR
          Welp too bad. You heard what the doctor
          said, you've been eating too much sugar.

                    MICHELLE
          I eat just the right amount of sugar.

                    JUNIOR
          One of these days you gonna listen to your
          big brother.

                    MICHELLE
            (Taking a sip)
          We're twins.

                    JUNIOR
          I'm still older.

                    MICHELLE
          By 2 minutes.

The crowd laughs again.

                    JUNIOR
          A win is a win.

Another small laugh comes from the crowd. MICHELLE
and JUNIOR take a sip from their lemonades and look
up and past the crowd.

                    MICHELLE
          How many of these do you think we've seen?

                    JUNIOR
Sunsets? I don't know. But it's always
beautiful.

                    MICHELLE
Do you remember the first time we watched
one of these?

                    JUNIOR
When we went fishing on the lake.

                    MICHELLE
That wasn't the first.

                    JUNIOR
It was the first.

                    MICHELLE
You must be starting to lose it.

                    JUNIOR
Well tell me genius when was the first time
we watched a sunset.

                    MICHELLE
We was at uncle Issac house and he was
cookin those nasty, stinkin 'chitlins and
we ran out to get air.

                    JUNIOR
          (Thinking)
YES YES. Now I remember.

                    MICHELLE
And when we ran outside the sky was just
beautiful.

They continue looking out. JUNIOR looks at MICHELLE,
she feels his eyes, and turns towards him.

                    MICHELLE
What's up?

                    JUNIOR
          I have a question for you.

MICHELLE sits up in her chair.

                    JUNIOR
          If you loved me today and the day before,
          would you love me tomorrow?

                    MICHELLE
          Of course, for eternity and every day
          after.

He reaches for her hand.

                    JUNIOR
          You're the best sister a man could ask for.

An awe comes from the crowd.

                    JUNIOR
          What was that song that was playing on the
          radio that day?

                    MICHELLE
          It wasn't no song you're making stuff up
          now.

                    JUNIOR
          It was on the radio,
               (Thinking)
          Oh my goodness what's the name of that
          song.
               (Still thinking)
          Oh my goodness I know it. Yes I got it.
          Hold on I'll be right back.

JUNIOR quickly staggers off the stage, getting a
laugh from the crowd because of how he's walking.
After a few beats he comes back, a vinyl record in
hand.

                    MICHELLE
          What song is it?

                    JUNIOR
          You're about to see.

He takes the vinyl out of the plastic, places it
down and drops the needle on it.

LIKE A STAR by CORINNE BAILEY RAE plays.

                    MICHELLE
              (Listening closely)
          I don't remember this.

                    JUNIOR
          What do you mean you don't remember?

                    MICHELLE
          I said what I said, I don't remember.

                    JUNIOR
          Come on get up.

                    MICHELLE
          Why would I do that?

                    JUNIOR
          Because we are now going to dance. Get up.

She sighs at first and then slowly stands up, JUNIOR
restarts the song.

He holds out his hand, she grabs it and comes closer
to him. The two dance slowly to RAE'S vocals.

We watch them dance, beginning to FADE back through
this year and the journey it took for them to get
here.

Them going to find the bullies who took JUNIOR'S
money; MICHELLE getting in her brother's face;
MICHELLE standing over JUNIOR while he is resting in
the hospital bed giving him a kiss on the cheek and
a hug; the pair in the country riding bikes, playing
badminton, modeling clothes, throwing rocks, and
MICHELLE resting her head on JUNIOR'S shoulders
watching the sunset.

These moments culminate to this, the two of them
dancing with such tranquil fluidity. On this stage
the audience is watching more than a show but a
rebirth. Two siblings proud to be in each other
arms, grateful to share the same DNA, happy that
they are able to share this moment and all the other
moments to come, TOGETHER.

FADE TO BLACK.

<u>END OF ACT IV: SPRING</u>

<u>END OF FILM</u>